CLUB LIFE

*The
Games
Golfers Play*

JOHN STEINBREDER

TAYLOR TRADE PUBLISHING
Lanham • New York • Boulder • Toronto • Oxford

Published by Taylor Trade Publishing
An imprint of The Rowman & Littlefield Publishing Group, Inc.
4501 Forbes Boulevard, Suite 200, Lanham, Maryland 20706

Distributed by NATIONAL BOOK NETWORK

Library of Congress Cataloging-in-Publication Data

Steinbreder, John.
    Club life : the games golfers play / John Steinbreder.—
    1st Taylor Trade Pub. ed.
        p. cm.
    ISBN-13: 978-1-58979-292-0 (cloth : alk. paper)
    ISBN-10: 1-58979-292-0 (cloth : alk. paper)
    1. Golf—Social aspects—United States. 2. Country clubs—
Social aspects—United States. 3. Golfers—United States—
Conduct of life. I. Title.
GV979.S63S84 2006
796.35206'873—dc22   2005035578

CONTENTS

ACKNOWLEDGMENTS

THE FIRST THING a writer wants to do when he finishes a volume like this is thank God, or whatever higher being he believes to exist. Then, he wants to show his gratitude to those mortals who helped him through what can only be described as a literary version of giving birth. Especially when he has had as much help in the delivery as I have with this, my seventh book.

My deep appreciation begins with my publisher Rick Rinehart of Rowman & Littlefield, who took a chance on this tome when others would not and showed great patience and perspective throughout the process.

Of course, there would not have even been a process if not for the generous support of my colleagues at *Golfweek*, editor Dave Seanor and publisher Jim Nugent. It was Dave who listened thoughtfully to my suggestion several years ago about the need for a regular column on life at golf and country clubs and then encouraged me to write it, even as it sometimes generated prodigious amounts of hate mail. And Jim not only lent support to that feature from the very beginning but was also the one who believed that publishing a book based on the columns was a good idea and did several things to make this a reality. Thanks, friends; once again, you have demonstrated why I think I have the best job in golf.

I also feel that way because of the many other people I work with at *Golfweek*. Bradley Klein is a good friend, a fair critic, and an insightful source, and I am always glad for his assistance in all my work. Gene Yasuda provides solid leadership and keen understanding as my frequent editor, as does Marty Kaufmann, who has just acquired the dubious distinction of becoming the next Club Life editor. And I would be remiss in not thanking the man who brought Club Life to life, Jeff Barr, who recently left *Golfweek* but only after carefully nurturing the column through the years as my editor and tightening my sometimes turgid prose.

A key component of any club is the PGA of America professional. They are the ones who run the golf programs and attend to the many needs—and often-mercurial whims—of their memberships. And it is almost impossible to properly appreciate what a difficult job they have, and how deftly they handle all that is thrown at them. I have been writing about this royal and ancient game almost exclusively for the past seven years, and among the very best people I have met in golf—and among the most helpful when it comes to understanding so many of its intricacies—have been those club pros. So, I would like to acknowledge the ones I know and respect best, among them Jack Druga, Bob Ford, Jim Langley, Brendan Walsh, Paul Marchand, Scott Nye, Mike Downey,

M. G. Orender, Jim Awtrey, Michael Breed, J. J. Weaver, Tony Sessa, Doug Steffen, Eric Schneider, Brannen Veal, Will Hutter, Chrissy Felton, Dennis Satyshur, Rob Anderson, Tim O'Neal, Sam Wiley, Eden Foster, Billy Anderson, Tony Pancake, Steve Friedlander, Ted Kiegiel, Brad Worthington, Tim Surlas, Mike Wright, and Charley Raudenbush.

And while the club pros are often the guys on the front lines, they are by no means the only ones taking shots. So, here's to the course superintendents who make the grasses green and the places we play so well conditioned. I am particularly grateful to Dave Koziol, Pat Sisk, and Jonathan Jennings for their help—and friendship—over the years, and they have made Connecticut for supers what the Dominican Republic town of San Pedro de Macoris is for major league baseball shortstops. In other words, a veritable breeding ground for the best the sport has to offer.

We in golf are very often blessed with the company of individuals whose love and knowledge of the game has no bounds, and they always seem willing to selflessly share their thoughts and feelings about issues affecting it. They are also great fun to play with and make any time together on the links pure joy. They are, to quote a friend, "great golf guys," and I would not have been able to do my work in this sport, or enjoy it quite as much, if not for them. My thanks, then, to Jim Stahl, Wally Uihlein, Herb Kohler, Hootie Johnson, Bill Jones, Glenn Greenspan,

ACKNOWLEDGMENTS

Richie Tilghman, Sam Reeves, Casey Alexander, Jerrett Garner, Todd Martin, Sean McManus, Josh Lesnik, Davis Love III, Scotty Cameron, Jack Vardaman, Eric Gleacher, Vinnie Giles, Tom Loss, Steve Smyers, John Bauman, Tom Crolius, Scott Mahoney, and David Abel.

And on a personal note, I would like to express my gratitude to Jim Dodson, David Owen, Michael Thomas, and Jim Nantz for penning those blurbs; John Akers for the great golf games at our favorite clubs; Nat and Owen Foote for our rounds together; Jerry Yang for the GIV, the Chateau Latour and all the giggles; Bill Gray for his wrinkle-free wear as well as his all-weather wit; and Duncan Christy for the great assignments over the years as well as those special games at Dinsmore National.

Finally, I need to thank my mother Cynthia Steinbreder for her unwavering support through yet another book project; my 14-year-old daughter Exa who continues to be the light of my life even as she demonstrates that dealing with a teenager is about as easy as hitting a flop shot off a hard-pan lie; and Cynthia Crolius, who has delightfully shown me that there are indeed things better than a weekend at Augusta National. Such as spending time with her.

John Steinbreder
Easton, Connecticut
November 2005

INTRODUCTION

THE GOLF CLUB may be most commonly regarded as a place where men and women play that royal and ancient game, but truth be told, it also serves as a sort of Petri dish for some of the most outrageous, hysterical, and inane behavior found in modern society. And Central Casting could not come up with a better collection of characters to act out those dramas and comedies. You have hackers and stiffs. Flakes and dilettantes. Corporate bigwigs and trust fund babies. They all exist in a kind of upper crust Animal House, where the denizens wear Burberry blazers instead of togas and guzzle gin-and-tonics rather than beer.

But the laughs, and head shaking, are very much the same.

Golf clubs exist as worlds of their own, mini-societies ruled in many cases by power-hungry leaders, populated by outspoken and often-ill-informed factions and beset with many of the same problems afflicting much larger efforts of human organization and activity. Throw in prodigious amounts of ego, plenty of money, regular infusions of liquor and the odd vendetta between long-feuding families, and you have an environment that produces as much emotional and personal dysfunction as it does good golf. It is theater at its very best, reality television without the cameras or pretension. It is club life, in its most honest form.

It is also something I have been closely observing the past several years in a regular column for *Golfweek* magazine called "Club Life," in which I describe the many things I see at the golf club to which I belong as well as those in other parts of the sporting world and opine on the degree of silliness—and occasionally small-mindedness—they reach. The results, I would like to think, are engaging pieces that strike chords among those of us who know and play the game because the issues, incidents, and characters are universal in nature and humorous to the core. They are also appealing because, quite frankly, you cannot make any of it up.

Club Life is about the lady who sends back a Bombay martini because it is "too strong," and the man who orders a tuna melt, "but without the cheese." It is the forty-something fellow clad mostly in Gucci and Hermes who talks about what a tough year he has had in the sort of accent one usually hears at Long Island polo games. "I got fired, I crashed my Mercedes and then my wife left me," he laments with a heavy sigh. "But things are looking up. I have a new job, and Mummy died."

It is also about the two fellows who hit their tee shots into the water of a par-3, right by the halfway house at their club and a place where golfers normally play for drinks and snacks bought at the turn, with the one ending up farthest from the pin paying the bill. Rather than gracefully splitting the tab after such abysmal drives, however, the seniors got into a terrific argument over whose Pinnacle went in to the drink closest to the hole. Ten minutes of intense haggling ensued, nearly bringing play to a standstill, and two old friends to blow. But cooler heads prevailed when a following foursome resolved the dispute by picking up the tab and sending the near-combatants on their way.

One of my favorite constituencies at any club are the rule breakers, the men and women who regularly skirts regulations that are supposed to govern behavior and keep the empire from falling apart. There is, for example, the deviant who cannot resist hitting practice balls off the range tee reserved for lessons. It doesn't matter that there is an obvious sign stating that the site is for the exclusive use of the pro and his students. Nor does it seem too important that the rest of the range is empty. This golfer thinks nothing about dumping a bucket of balls on that tee and hitting one double-striper after another until he has shaved off a vast section of sod the size of a manhole cover. It drives the pro crazy but bothers the rule bender not one bit.

Another version of this group is the fellow who delights in bringing a pile of out-of-towners to a club's beach section without paying the appropriate guest fees. This is a man who married so well he could afford to buy half his hometown. But damn if he will pay the $5-a-head charge for each nonmember, no matter what the rules say. What he does instead is lie to the guard at the security gate, hiding his guests in the back of his SUV as if they were illegal immigrants being smuggled across the border. When he makes his way past the checkpoint and parks by the beach, people start pouring out of his vehicle, like clowns out of a circus car.

A person could argue, of course, that club rules, whether written or merely understood, can be witless, capricious and completely unworthy of consideration or adherence. And I can see some logic in that thinking. After all, is the sky going to fall if a male golfer dons a pair of short shorts or a mock T shirt, no matter how hideous it may look? And will a fivesome on a slow weekday morning in the fall bring riots to the street and dishonor to the fiefdom?

Not necessarily. But the fact is, a club needs order to function properly, and order is best maintained by a strict and sensible set of rules. And in order to be effective, those rules have to be enforced on a regular and consistent basis. Otherwise, chaos reigns, and that seemingly charming place we go for our games of golf and our rounds of drinks suddenly become Groucho Marx's stateroom in *A Night at the Opera*.

Fortunately, many people in golf understand that, and there is no doubt that the best golf clubs in the land are those run most strictly, usually by despots who rule with an iron will—and fist—paying little heed to the whims and wants of those they rule.

Personally, I like the feel of a good golf dictatorship. Maybe it's because I am half-German and turning slowly into my father, who ran his household the way Clifford Roberts ran Augusta National and once told me after a trip to South Korea in the 1970s that he liked Seoul because it had tanks in the streets at night. It could also be that the most despotic retreats are the only ones that really get the joke and seem to get everything right, from having strong caddie programs and generous bartenders to locker-room attendants who replace the broken Softspikes in your shoes without being asked and remember your name after only one day. And no one ever steps out of line.

A good example is Pine Valley, where the late John Arthur Brown long served as president. One day, he got so exercised at a plodding foursome that he drove out to the course in his golf cart to confront the group. Instead of going up to the golfers themselves, who were standing on the 13th tee, he approached the caddies, who were waiting in the fairway, and said: "That's enough, boys. Pick up those bags and take them back to the clubhouse." Then off he drove, leaving the offending players with a rather long walk back in, and some very strong revelations about proper pace of play.

The most famous club dictator of all time was Roberts, and the best-known demonstration of his leadership philosophy involved a pine tree off the left side of the 17th fairway at Augusta. Roberts was presiding over a board of governors meeting in 1956, and Dwight Eisenhower, who happened to be our nation's president at the time, suggested the club cut down the tree. Roberts immediately ruled Augusta's most famous member out of order and adjourned the meeting. And the pine stayed right where it was.

Another of the great golf dictators was Mrs. Joseph V. Reed of the Jupiter Island Club in Hobe Sound, Florida. Mrs. Reed's family owned the land on which the club was built, and she ruled it like an impatient empress. One of her tactics was having people photographed in the act of committing infractions, such a wearing a collarless shirt on the course, and then sending them a copy of the image with a terse letter of admonishment. If you got more than a letter or two like that, it was probably time to move off the island.

Jupiter members feared Mrs. Reed more than the taxman and would submit to almost any embarrassment to avoid getting on her bad side. Like the friend of mine who was putting on the 18th green one winter afternoon when one of Mrs. Reed's small dogs wrapped himself around the golfer's leg in what can only be described as an amorous embrace. The man tried to shed the overfriendly canine by fiercely shaking his leg but froze instantly when Mrs. Reed called out from her nearby cart: "Stop kicking my dog."

People sometimes asked me how I have come to know golf clubs as I do, and the answer is fairly simple. For starters, I grew up around them. My parents joined one in Connecticut when I was 6 years old, and I spent a fair amount of time there during the summers of my youth, playing tennis, going swimming and, only occasionally in those days, hitting golf balls. We also visited other clubs on a fairly regular basis, as many of our family's friends belonged to ones of their own.

Then, clubs became important parts of my adult life. I eventually joined that spot in Connecticut in my mid-20s, when age dictated that I could no longer mooch under my parent's membership, and found it was a great place to recreate when the workweek was over. Around that same time, I discovered the need to schmooze sources and interact with contacts in my work as a journalist often forced me to patronize other golf and country clubs on a fairly regular basis. Then, I began writing for *Golfweek*, and suddenly the course—and club—truly became a place of business for me. By that time, it had also become an intensely important spot for me to relax and socialize, as my love for golf grew along with the number of friends who found similar joy in gathering at that kind of retreat.

Not surprisingly, the more time I spent at golf clubs, the more I learned about the senseless, maddening, and frequently shocking things that so often went down at those spots, whether it was from listening to a pair of members talking in the locker room and a couple gossiping over lunch or after talking to a general manager who wanted to share his frustrations at the end of a long day and fellow golfers who chatted during our rounds. Some things I picked up at my place, where I had begun to assume a variety of leadership positions that gave me even greater—and many times unwanted—access to the ridiculous and absurd. And the rest of it came from those away rounds of golf I played all over the world, from California to Morocco, and Australia to Georgia. What struck me more than anything was how similar the experience and feelings were no matter where I teed it up. And I eventually began doing what writers often do in their lives, which is take notes of the things I observed with the express purpose of distilling the best material into pieces that would find their way in print.

That's how the Club Life column was born.

Occasionally, I am asked if I have any real motivation for composing those pieces, many of which are highly opinionated, somewhat edgy, usually irreverent and invariably enraging to certain readers. Generally speaking, my response is threefold. First, I have an inherent frustration with what I believe is a general trend toward boorish behavior around a golf club, especially as it relates to members treating not only each other badly but also the staff that serves them so faithfully. There are fits of arrogance, belligerence, and outright meanness that didn't exist a couple decades ago and an overwhelming sense in some circles that the numbers detailing a member's net worth are often confused with their IQ. And people seem far too willing to ignore some of the most basic forms of good golf club etiquette, whether it is taking off your hat when you walk inside a clubhouse or not using a cell phone on the grounds. As a result, I take certain delight in exposing such wrongheaded Neanderthals, if only to themselves. I must also confess to an unrealistic hope that maybe those sorts of deadbeats can be shamed into forsaking their errant ways, but I have come to understand that still is a pipe dream. However, dreams do die hard, and that is a difficult one for me to let go of.

Besides, sticking a finger in a miscreant's eye can feel pretty good.

I am also driven by an intense delight in flattening sacred cows, thumbing my nose at political correctness, and enjoying whatever opportunity I have to deflate those people whose misguided self-importance on the club level can absolutely ruin whatever good those places provide. There is nothing quite so gratifying as writing a piece on the virtues of men's grillrooms and getting two dozen e-mails the day after it ran from people who act as if I had suggested that women should be denied all access to the golf course and the only sort of proper attire for distaff duffers is a burka. Once I wrote a tongue-in-cheek story in the days heading up to the 2003 U.S. Open, which was being played at the Olympia Fields Golf Club outside Chicago, averring that the Windy City truly was the Second City when it came to golf and stating that New York was best. And suddenly I received a collection of acerbic rantings that not only questioned my intellect and lineage but also made me out to be some horrid cross between Richard Speck and Sammy Sosa.

Gee, you would have thought I said Michael Jordan was a gambler.

But most of what motivates me when it comes to Club Life is the fun I have, laughing at myself and so many of those around me, as we go about our golfing lives at these wonderful places. Because as aggravating and impossible as much of it can be, it is also so laughable. I split my sides when I think of my friend's comments that golf carts have done to the game what P Diddy and Britney Spears have done to music. Or his thought that he will never live long enough for any of these new golf courses being built across this land to be any good. I chuckle at the suggestion once made over post-round drinks that the staff at any golf club should be allowed to throw out one member a year. Or the time some guys at my place hung a sign in the locker of our new greens chairman that read: "Get the geese, or we are going to get you." I also get a kick out of Willie Nelson's story about dressing up in a skirt and halter top so he could adhere to the dress code policy of a club he played in Florida.

Finally, I love the tale about the New England club that not too long ago looked into renovating its clubhouse. When the price soared too high for those old-line Yankees, they started scrounging for ways to cut back. One suggestion: instead of replacing the floorboards of the expansive porch, which had been pockmarked with spike marks, they would simply flip over the wood and use the other side. It sounded good to one and all, but when workers turned over the first boards they found the previous club leaders had had the same idea some decades ago.

Great stuff, to be sure. And you truly cannot make any of it up.

WHAT MAKES
A CLUB GREAT

THE QUESTION is one my friends and I often ponder after a round, and it really is quite simple: What makes a golf club great?

The obvious first answer is that a great golf club must have a great golf course. But there are many other factors involved.

A great golf club has small scorecards, primarily white and about the size of a playing card when folded, and not illustrated with photographs. Like Augusta National's. Pencils with erasers are a nice touch as well.

A great golf club also has a small but well-appointed pro shop, and the 1st tee is just a short walk away, which is what you'll find at Cypress Point and Riviera. It is a place that has a fabulous porch (Shinnecock) and at least one signature drink (Southsides, again at Shinnecock) or dish (snapper soup at Pine Valley, or perhaps freshly cooked lobster at the National Golf Links). But the food never comes close to overshadowing the course, and there is never any question that the most important hires are always the head professional or course superintendent and not the pastry chef. You talk about the quality of the layout and the joy of the golfing experience when you leave, not the lunchtime buffet. And it doesn't matter if you ever have an actual dinner at the club. Golf remains the focus of the association, and members recognize that most club eateries function about as well financially as the Argentine economy and bleed gallons of red ink for what often is some of the worst food in town. They also appreciate that club restaurants frequently detract attention from the course and also serve to attract members who don't care as much about the game and might concern themselves more with the entrees that make up a 15-course brunch buffet.

The exception to the above rule, of course, is those clubs, like Augusta, that take in a lot of overnight guests and have people staying on the premises for two or three days. In those cases, a first-rate dining facility is an understandable necessity. And so is a well-stocked wine cellar.

A great golf club has a strong caddie program, a small fleet of golf carts that are available only to those who have legitimate medical excuses, and a head professional who got his or her start in the caddie shack or bag room. It is the sort of spot where touring pros and top amateurs play on their days off.

A great golf club does not have to institute a "No Cell Phone" policy because the membership is so old that no one has a cell phone or knows how to operate one; and even if they did, it would never occur to them to bring one onto the course. It is also where you will find an honor system at the practice range and at the halfway house. Members at clubs like that have no interest in cheating each other out of a few bucks.

Speaking of halfway houses, a great golf club has only the most austere setup for those mid-round breaks. It does not have monstrous walk-in refrigerators or ultra-modern hot dog grills, but rather the simplest selections of drinks and snacks, and maybe even a day-old sandwich or two. After all, we are only talking about a four-hour round at most, not a five-day desert march, and it seems ridiculous to need—or want— much more.

A great golf club still has a men's grillroom, no matter how politically incorrect that may be, and is the sort of place that might require a jacket in the bar but no clothes on the course (such as Garden City, where members can play in the nude for all they care). It also has a place in the locker room where you can sit and have drinks after your rounds. All the flags on the greens are the same color (yes, you have to figure out where the pins are by yourself) and there are no GPS systems or yardage markers. It is also a spot that is so old and traditional that it can no longer host a U.S. Open either because it lacks parking, length, or the inclination to be overrun by hordes of golf fans—and the United States Golf Association—just for a little extra money and recognition. But it would be happy to take on a Walker Cup, or some similarly prominent but low-key amateur event.

A great golf club has only a short walk between greens and tees (Cypress Point, again) and a course designed by an architect who long ago went on to his great reward (such as Charles Blair Macdonald, Seth Raynor, A. W. Tillinghast, Alister Mackenzie, or Donald Ross). And at some point during your round, you play one of the great holes from the British Isles, whether it's a Redan, Road, Postage Stamp, or Eden.

Great golf clubs do not have swimming pools. Or if they do, they are completely unused, as is the case with the one at Seminole. They also forsake tennis courts, understanding the importance of having places that are only—and unabashedly—about golf. As a result, the membership is more focused about what it wants, and there is a greater commonality of interest and purpose. Different factions divide no one, and no one is distracted from the thing that kindled creation of the club itself. Which, of course, was golf.

You see, it is a fact of club life that a sort of one-upmanship occurs whenever the finance committee starts doling out money at budget time, and as soon as it reveals its allocations for the golf course, some disenfranchised group of swimmers will inevitably start screaming about getting their fair share for larger lockers, perhaps, or fluffier towels.

Great golf clubs also have very small or inactive memberships, so the courses are almost always empty and the pace of play delightfully quick. I played 36 holes at Chicago Golf Club last fall with two other fellows in just over six hours, without even stopping between rounds. And the one time I teed it up at San Francisco Golf Club, I saw only one other group on the course. On a Saturday afternoon, no less, and it was a fivesome that finished in less than four hours.

A great golf club understands just how special an experience it offers first-timers and makes a point of treating its guests as well as its members. That's one of the things that make Augusta National and Cypress Point so good. And greatness must be bestowed on any club that is able to maintain the same feel and character over the years. Like this venerable spot I know in New England that not too long ago looked into renovating its clubhouse. When the estimated price soared too high for those old-line Yankees, they started scrounging for ways to cut back. One suggestion: Instead of replacing the floorboards of the expansive porch, which had been pocked with spike marks, they would simply flip over the wood and use the other side. It sounded good to one and all, but when workers turned over the first boards, they found the previous club leaders had had the same idea some decades before.

As for the name of that wonderful place, it is something readers are going to have to do without, because the club boasts one other element that makes it, and those like it, great. And that is having utter disdain or ambivalence when it comes to publicity.

I long ago determined that the presence of train tracks frequently is a sign of great golf. Think of Royal Adelaide in South Australia, with its commuter line rolling through that wonderful layout, which Mackenzie tweaked during his historic trip Down Under nearly a century ago. Or Pine Valley in southern New Jersey, where the rumble of a freight train through the sandy woods late on a summer afternoon is only one more reason to fawn over that fabulous retreat. Even the one-time presence of rail lines (St. Andrews) or the proximity of tracks and the sound of, say, an engine's whistle (such as Dunbar in East Lothian) often means the course itself will be sweet.

Strange as it may seem, airports can also be an indication of a quality layout. I first came to that conclusion while playing Royal Dublin and Royal Portmarnock in Ireland, and it was only reinforced after a trip to Australia a few years later, and a lovely round at New South Wales Golf Club, during which I got to watch several 747s take off from Sydney's airport and climb into the wind. I sometimes get that same sensation in the States, whether I am teeing it up at a place such as North Shore Country Club outside Chicago or Blind Brook, which is near the White Plains airport in New York's Westchester County.

I have long had a theory with restaurants that you can judge the quality of an eatery by the size of the pepper mill, the idea being, the larger the mill, the worse the restaurant. And I have developed a similar premise about golf clubs, believing that the smaller or more obscure the entrance sign, the better the course and club. Much of that stems from my liking a place that is so secure it does not feel a need to trumpet its location. That's most definitely the case with San Francisco Golf, and there is something beguiling about a club that first-time visitors may pass by once or twice before finally finding their way in. The thought, of course, is that a special spot often needs to be unearthed before it can truly be enjoyed.

And if a sign is a must, then I am keen on the way Chicago Golf handles it, with a name board so obscure and difficult to see as you pull up to the club drive that it might as well not be there at all.

When it comes to clubhouses, I prefer structures that are small, simple, and feel more like quaint abodes than the types of overblown wedding halls that seem to be all the rage in some circles today. Those that straddle opening holes, such as Merion's, are wonderful for players and spectators alike, so long as none of the golfers go sideways with their first shots. And I am big on clubhouses that overlook the finishing hole and afford golfers sipping their post-round quaffs the opportunity to watch others finish. That's one of the best things about the 18th at Garden City on Long Island, and also the Country Club of Fairfield on the Connecticut coast.

Another asset of any great golf retreat is the ability for guests to transfer charges to their home club, which Cypress allows. I also like spots, like Cypress, that have rooms for out-of-town members and their guests. A night or two in a place like that can be sweet, especially as you coddle a late-night cognac on the edge of your bed and listen to sea lions bark from their rocky lairs off the 17th tee, knowing you have plans for 36 holes the following day.

I have long held affection for clubs that not only have caddie programs but also caddie scholarship trusts. Or at the very least, provide important financial support to regional foundations that help loopers make their way through college. There is also lots to like about spots where members linger happily at the 19th hole after their games, not simply to drink but also to relish each other's company in settings that are all about golf. Even better are places where the game and ambiance is so revered that members often jump in carts when they are done playing—and finished with their first round of drinks—to go out and watch friends make their way in.

These days, I find myself favoring clubs that keep all signage to a minimum. Frankly, I always have felt that less is more on any course, which is why I love places that use only the most basic tee markers (such as those little pieces of wood at Pine Valley), eschew ball washers (because caddies will take care of that task), and forget about putting litter baskets at every tee (because it is just as easy for a player to stuff any garbage he finds or accumulates in his pocket or bag until the round is over). The idea, of course, is to eliminate as many potential eye sores as possible and make a layout as visually enticing as it is fun to play.

But I seem to be a glutton for field grass that turns such a wonderful brown in the late summer in my part of the world, and moves like waves in the morning wind. In addition, I never worry about too much bird or wildlife. Turkeys frequently roam the fairways of my place, and we often see cottontail rabbits, pheasants, ducks, red-tail hawks, and the odd fox or coyote. Many times, my friends and I are treated to the glorious sight of a kingfisher diving headlong into one of our water hazards to snatch a bite to eat, or sea gulls dropping clams on the beach road that runs along our second and third fairways, using the asphalt to break open mollusks for their daily repast, and that never fails to take the sting out of a bad score. The waterfowler in me even enjoys the Canada geese. I know their presence irks large contingents of golfers, but I never feel the birds do as much damage to our track as to warrant such unwavering disdain. And the pleasure I get in watching them trade back and forth on a weekend morning more than offsets the occasional dismay at some droppings on a green.

I know that bigger seems to be better in the golf world these days, but I have high regard for the places that do not feel the need to stretch themselves out to absurd lengths to accommodate the prodigious driving distances of a minuscule percentage of players. Better to tighten the fairways, perhaps. Or grow the rough. Or add a few strategic bunkers. And what's wrong with even shortening a course on occasion by building forward tees on some holes to give them much different—and often more difficult—perspective?

That sort of philosophy also has me praising golf courses where par is 70; it seems a quaint number that harkens back to a lower testosterone time, when all par-4s did not have to be 450 yards, and no one had a heart attack if you occasionally hit a wedge for an approach shot.

Besides, I like the fact that you can be nine over par on a track like that and still break 80, which is my goal every time I walk onto a course.

I must also confess an unrepentant bias to layouts of a certain age. And that emotion reminds me of something my friend Jenkins said after he spent a golf holiday playing several highly rated modern tracks.

"I am not going to live long enough for any of these new courses to be any good," he sighed.

I chuckled heartily at that comment, for it mirrored something noted golf architect Tom Doak wrote in the Foreword of George Bahto's compelling book on Charles Blair Macdonald, "The Evangelist of Golf."

"Some people prefer older women," he penned. "I prefer older courses."

To be sure, there are several modern layouts that tickle my fancy, chief among them the three courses in Bandon Dunes, Oregon (one of which, Pacific Dunes, Doak designed), the Straits course at Herb Kohler's golfing paradise in Wisconsin, and Bill Jones's superb Ocean Forest in Sea Island, Georgia. But they are much more the exception than the rule, and when I am forced to choose where I want to play, I almost always opt for the more seasoned layouts.

Why? Let's start with the fact that older courses often were built on the very best pieces of property, mainly because they came into being first and good land was relatively cheap and easy to acquire back then. Therefore, they have the most interesting terrain with all the views, contours, elevation changes, and diversity that make great layouts great.

I also find an appealing maturity to those types of tracks and a pleasing sense that they have been there for a while and aged quite nicely, like a fine bottle of port. Generally speaking, they possess a wonderfully modest subtlety to their designs because they were put together by architects who did not have the technological means to move a lot of earth and had to deal with what the Good Lord gave them.

In addition, they rarely were as pressured as modern designers to come up with 18 signature holes on any one course and overreach in an attempt to bolster their reputations and justify their fees. And in many cases, those aged tracks boast a compelling heritage that can be delightfully recounted with each round. Perhaps Marion Hollins and Francis Ouimet played there with a member in the 1920s, or Billy Casper competed in an exhibition with a local pro a month before he won the U.S. Open.

I also liked the fact that most older courses utilize smaller parcels of land than the newer tracks, giving them a sense of efficient beauty and deft design. And I appreciate how some of those venerable layouts can get away with eschewing such modern necessities as, say, an irrigation system, or at the very least one that douses every square foot of land. Yes, the green grass of a well-watered track often does look beautiful, but a true links is to be played on the ground and in the brown. There is a terrific elegance and quality to that look that most current course owners and builders would not allow for fear of scaring off potential members or players.

Older courses are generally part of older clubs, and those are usually much more attractive retreats than there younger counterparts. The ones that have been around since the Jazz Age, for example, often have a charming history as well as staff members—be they longtime locker-room attendants or hoary head pros—who have worked there for years and give it a special flavor. In addition, I find the newer clubs frequently loosen admission standards to make sure they fill their pricey rolls, and that leads to difficult memberships. That sort of situation is of great concern to Jenkins, and he tells me that while he could afford to pay $300,000 for an annual membership to one of those places, he would rather quit the game than endure the kind of aggravation that is apt to exist there.

You see, old clubs rarely get people who try to change the essence of the game as it is played at those spots, or the nature of the club. And their membership ranks are generally filled with folks who know each other, which leads to a more comfortable social fabric and more compatible operations. However, many of those newer spots, which have been predicated on attracting a high net worth membership, lack that sort of tradition due to their young age and do not have that kind of cohesiveness because money is not exactly a unifying factor—in golf or anything else.

They say that youth is wasted on the young, but when it comes to golf, it is often wasted on me as well. Give me something with a little age.

It's just one more thing that helps make a club great.

BEST OF SHOW

EVERY SPRING, *Golfweek* magazine puts out a ranking of the best modern and classic golf courses in America, as determined by a cadre of some 350 raters who traverse the country, clubs slung over their backs, to assess courses of all ilks and configurations. As a senior writer for that publication, I use the occasion to assemble a roster of what I think is great in other aspects of the game, and the following choices are distilled from weeks of rigorous samplings of as many of these wonderful retreats as time would allow. It is an ugly job, to be sure, but someone has to do it.

BEST ENTRANCE: Cypress Point Club. Off scenic 17-Mile Drive and shaded by glorious hardwoods, this ingress leads to one of the best—and most exclusive layouts—in the world. No guardhouse, no traffic, and only a modest sign. So heavenly is the sense of arrival that you half-expect St. Peter to wave you in.

BEST RANGE: The gold standard in this realm is Pine Valley Golf Club, where the practice area seems as big as Delaware and often has been the place where sleek corporate helicopters alight, coolly discharging their golfing passengers before lifting off into the sky. But my favorite is the one at Fisher's Island, because there really isn't one. What players looking to limber up must do instead is bang their shag balls off a craggy ledge near the putting green into Barley Field Cove.

Another range worth noting is the one at the Merit Club in Chicago, largely because it includes three separate practice holes. And the newly built Frederica Golf Club in Sea Island, Georgia, has the best short game area I've ever seen, with plenty of places to work on shots from 120 yards and in.

BEST LOCKER ROOM (OTHER THAN SEMINOLE'S): The one at Bill Jones's Ocean Forest Golf Club in Sea Island is modeled after the facilities at that venerable Florida retreat, right down to the Big Game trophies adorning the walls. It's as cozy as your grandfather's den, and as well appointed as a suite at the Ritz. Plus, the guys who serve drinks and shine shoes have a marvelous habit of remembering names even if months go by between visits.

BEST PORCH: Shinnecock Hills in Southampton, N.Y., is among the finest in this department. And sitting outside of this Stanford White structure on a clear afternoon is almost as pleasurable as a round of golf at the

Long Island track. And much less taxing. Equally as good is the so-called Birdcage at neighboring National Golf Links, from which members and their guests can watch players come up the 18th hole as summer breezes gently blow and the waters of Peconic Bay shimmer in the distance. But my top choice is Country Club of Fairfield in Connecticut, which boasts a stunning view of the Seth Raynor golf course as well as Long Island Sound. On a clear day pre-9/11, you could make out the outlines of the World Trade Center towers some 50 miles away.

BEST PORCH DRINK: Southsides at Shinnecock. Or rum floats at Country Club of Fairfield, especially when Tony, Victor, and Winston get a little heavy-handed with the Goslings.

BEST LOGO: Among the older clubs, I love the fox head at Myopia Hunt Club in South Hamilton, Massachusetts, and the jagged island of Fisher's Island. And neither have had any names or lettering around them, which is always a nice touch. As for the moderns, I have to go with the puffin of Bandon Dunes and the seals of its sister course, Pacific Dunes. Fun, colorful, and simple.

BEST LOGO THAT LOOKS LIKE THE GUY WHO BUILT THE COURSE: Whistling Straits, whose image of a wild and windswept gnome bears a striking resemblance to Herb Kohler, the visionary who is the money and inspiration behind the excellent track on Lake Michigan.

BEST OUTLAW LOOP: The first five holes at Spyglass, played twice. I did that with one of the pros there late one afternoon, and it was a gas, for those are the seaside holes with the Pacific Ocean views and my favorite by far. We both looked at each other after finishing No. 5, and quickly decided that instead of heading into the Del Monte Forest on the 6th, we would return to play the opening quintet again. Sheer joy, and if the sun had not been going down, we would have done it a third time. Golf's version of Groundhog Day.

BEST WAIT STAFF: The Bear's Club in North Palm Beach, Florida. I teed it up there shortly after it had opened a few years ago, when lunch was served in the halfway house while the clubhouse was being built. I heard a high-pitched voice as I got ready to dig into my chicken salad and looked up to find Jack Nicklaus serving my iced tea. And no, he did not spill a drop.

BEST WINE CELLAR: Mayacama Golf Club in Santa Rosa, California, wins the prize for the superlative stash it holds in its 37,000-square-foot, Tuscan-style clubhouse. There are 400 individual wine lockers that can handle as much as 2 cases each, and the club has secured

25 special vintner memberships for those active in the wine business, with the understanding that they will provide, at cost, a barrel—or case equivalent—of their best wine each year to the club. Runner-up is Augusta National, which has a brilliantly stocked and moderately priced collection that boasts approximately 30,000 bottles, all neatly arrayed in a space below the Trophy Room.

BEST RESTAURANT NEAR A CLUB: The Reef Grill in Juno Beach, Florida, just down the road from the Seminole Golf Club. Incomparable seafood. Pleasing wine list. Enticing ambience. And don't be surprised if you see a number of club members, as well as some of Seminole's golf professionals, dining there. Another winner is Casanova's in the center of Carmel, California, just a short hop down 17-Mile Drive from Pebble Beach and Cypress Point. It's a fabulous place to retire for a glass of wine and a bite to eat after a round.

BEST STATUE: This selection is offered under the theory that barring extraordinary circumstances, no self-respecting golf course should ever have a statue. But the one of Charles Blair Macdonald outside the pro shop at Chicago Golf Club is a reasonable exception. After all, he was the founder and designer of the layout, which was the first 18-hole course, built in the United States and an original member of the United

States Golf Association. Plus, he won the 1895 U.S. Amateur and went on to create some of the finest courses in the land, most notably the National Golf Links. It also doesn't hurt that he was one of the game's great characters.

BEST PUTTING GREEN: The one at Congressional Country Club outside Washington is laid out on a sumptuous piece of turf that sits in the middle of the driveway circle in front of the majestic clubhouse. And though the place has everything from tennis courts to bowling lanes, the presence of that modest practice facility in such a prominent spot tells all comers that more than anything else, Congressional is about golf.

BEST PARKING LOT: Cypress Point gets the nod here, in part because it is so ridiculously close to the 1st tee, and often ridiculously empty. Tom Fazio once suggested the club move part of it back, but members firmly rejected the idea. Equally as good is the gravel lot at Seminole, where Jimmy the attendant arranges Bentleys and BMWs in perfect order, their shiny grills pointing out at an angle from the pick-walled clubhouse, each one with an Indian head license plate.

BEST CLUBHOUSE: The two-story, 40,000-square-foot, Tudor-style structure at East Lake Golf Club in Atlanta, where developer Tom Cousins has restored a museum-quality shrine to Bobby Jones at what was his home club, and at the same time showed golf how the game really can be used to make a difference in people's lives.

BEST LUNCH SPOT: Dining at one of those umbrella-shaded tables on the lawn outside the back of the clubhouse at Ekwanok Country Club in Manchester, Vermont, is one of the real treats in golf, especially as they overlook almost the entire Walter Travis course winding through a spacious valley. A great view turns downright spectacular in the fall when the maple leaves turn.

THE DARK SIDE

AS ANYONE who swings a 9-iron will attest, there is much to love about the game of golf. But it has a dark side, too, something I've found at courses and clubs across the land. Humans are amazingly adept at messing up what is as pure and delightful a recreation that exists in this world. They simply cannot leave well enough alone. And they not only change the very feel and nature of the sport as a result, but also irritate me to such extremes that I am compelled to compile a list of things I hate about golf.

And this is not a game I want to hate in any way.

Let's start with the first scene many of us encounter when we drive in to the entrances of those high-end, daily-fee courses that became all the rage in the 1990s. That, of course, is the horde of khaki-clad attendants descending upon the car with the same frenzied verve as those guys with squeegees who used to work the West Side stoplights in Manhattan. Initially, it feels like a mugging, then you have the sense of being herded, so much so that I half expect those efficacious greeters to brandish cattle prods if things don't move along quickly enough.

Then, we have the electronic equipment every employee seems to be wearing, the headsets and micro- phones they use to communicate with "command cen- tral." It makes them look like back-up singers at a Madonna concert, and makes me feel as if I am in the midst of a low-rent action movie (and about to storm the mountain lair with the Special Ops squad). Or going by the drive-thru station at Mickey D's.

And what's not to abhor about those tedious shot- gun tournaments where a pro shop worker assembles players around a sound system and advises everyone through a wireless mike of the various rules and regu- lations. The nonsensical—and usually interminable— discourse just about taps the last pang of enthusiasm for my day as I listen to the muffled voice of a chatty, lounge-singing wannabe carry across the verdant track I am supposed to be playing. Quite obviously, it is not the sound or setting I had hoped to experience.

Nor are the carts, which have done to golf what P Diddy and Britney Spears have done to music. Now, I understand the need for E-Z-GOs among those who are infirm or on enough in years that a little man-made transportation makes it easier—and more possible—for them to tee it up. But golf is a game that is meant to be walked by all others, and the only thing more unat- tractive than a pair of healthy 30-year-olds in one of those vehicles is the sight of a golf cart fleet all charged and ready to go.

Actually, it is even worse watching them go, which is something my friend Jenkins was reminded of during a member-guest at a lovely oceanside course last fall. He and a colleague were about to tee off and had taken a moment to admire the vista across the fairways, greens, and fescue rough when they turned their eyes to see more than a dozen carts cruising past in formation. "We had this great view of this great course, and then all of a sudden, the place looked like a potato farm," he says.

Carts in and of themselves also have created a whole subset of things to dislike. Such as courses you cannot walk or take a caddie on. I also have utter disdain for cart paths and those layouts that seemed lined with more pavement than the Mall of America. If you have to have a place to drive those battery-powered abominations, at least use crushed seashells.

Another problem is all the things that now come with carts. Like GPS systems, which not only mete out the mileage on each hole but also provide sports scores and halfway house menu options. I understand exact yardages can help unfamiliar golfers on resort courses, but isn't that what caddies are for? And who really cares about the Giants while you were out playing a Sunday round? Or putting in for a four-course meal at the turn? Stay home if the game—or the lunch—is that important, and please don't make me feel like I have to watch "Sports Center" between shots.

Then, there are those electric pull carts that either lead or follow golfers around their courses. To be fair, I do appreciate the fact that players employing those are indeed walking—and not riding—and I see how the introduction of vehicles allows golfers who are farther along the back nine of their lives to stave off the inevitable move to more traditional—and more irritating—carts. But nether Jenkins nor I can fathom why someone who is still capable of walking three or four miles of fairway does not have the physical inclination to pull his, or her, own cart along the way.

And I must admit to a certain fantasy each time I see one of those pull carts, in which it actually turns on its master and chases him into the mire of a water hazard or bunker before motoring off in triumph, free at last from the chains of mechanical caddying.

As for other items on my roster of wrongs, I might also include water hazards that have fountains and practice range balls arranged in the shape of pyramids (both too much like Las Vegas). Flowerbeds look terrible on any course but Augusta National, and the sort of man-made mounding you find on many new layouts is just as distasteful. Some designers feel the need to create "signature trees" on their tracks, and I'd just as soon have them take a chain saw to those obtrusive beauties.

I would also like to say good-bye to yardage books that require an advanced degree in engineering to understand, clubhouses that double as catering halls, and courses that have so many painted signs of instruction and advice by the 1st and 10th tees that they resemble one of those billboard-strewn highways out West. Golf bags that can only be carried by Olympic weightlifters are also worth chucking, as are those sheets that divide the greens by quadrants and provide pin placements. Again, isn't that something the golfer, and his caddie, should be figuring out for themselves?

More recently, I have developed an intense aversion to railroad ties, born largely from a visit last spring to a fairly new golf resort that had so many of those clunky wood logs it could have passed for a freight yard. And I still do not understand why anyone ever thought those ties were such a good idea when it comes to course construction. It seems that in the vast majority of cases, they have about as much business being on a quality golf layout as cinder blocks or aluminum siding, and I've always found that the more of them you find on a golf course, the worse the layout—or club—actually is.

As anyone who has spent any time around a golf club knows, each institution has its share of characters. There are hackers and flakes, dilettantes and stiffs, and it is never difficult dividing up the membership rolls by these—and other—categories. It is also easy to come up with new classifications, and the latest one I've added to my list is: Rule Benders. And they can ruin a day at a club as quickly as a late summer thunderstorm.

Quite simply, Rule Benders are those who regularly skirt regulations that are supposed to govern club behavior. They are not necessarily bad people, and there is nothing dangerously destructive about their actions. But they have a hard time following certain precepts.

Take the deviant I know who cannot resist hitting practice balls off the range tee reserved for lessons. It doesn't matter that there is a sign stating the site is for the exclusive use of the pros and their students. Nor does it seem important that the rest of the range often is empty. This golfer thinks nothing about dumping a bucket of balls on the tee and hitting one double-striper after the other until he has shaved off a vast section of sod. It drives the pros crazy, but bothers the Rule Bender not one bit, even when club leaders chastise him.

There is also the member at my place who delights in bringing a pile of out-of-towners to the club's beach section without paying the appropriate guest fees. This is the man who married so well he can afford to buy half my hometown. But damned if he will pay the $5-a-head charge for each nonmember, no matter what the rules say. What he does instead is lie to the guard at the security gate, hiding his guests in the back of his SUV as if they were illegal immigrants being smuggled across the border. When he makes his way past the checkpoint and parks by the beach, people start pouring out of his vehicle like clowns out of a circus car.

Over the years, I have found there are three types of Rule Benders. First is the longtime club member who feels he has been around for so many years that none of the laws and tenets applies to him anymore. Then, there is the newcomer who is so wealthy, arrogant, and self-absorbed that he doesn't think any rules apply to him. Finally, we have your basic rebel, the golfer who can take only so much authority and feels he is not really living if he is not crossing the line in some way, shape, or form.

One could argue, of course, that club rules—whether written or merely understood—often are silly, capricious, and completely unworthy of consideration (or adherence). And there is some logic to that type of thinking. I mean, is the empire really going to crumble if a male golfer dons a pair of short shorts? Will a fivesome on a slow weekday afternoon bring riots to the streets and dishonor to the fiefdom?

But the fact is, a club needs order to function properly, and order is best maintained by a strict and sensible set of rules.

Those edicts, however, get in the way of the Rule Bender, and the lengths to which he goes to circumvent them would be hilarious if they were not so annoying.

I've found that the practice range is perhaps the most fertile ground for that type of behavior. In addition to those who hit balls off the lesson tee, there are golfers who seem psychologically incapable of smacking their woods and irons from the designated section of turf set off by nylon ropes. To those members, the grass truly is greener on the other side, and that's where they hit most of their balls—exactly where the head professional and course superintendent wish they wouldn't.

I also marvel at the true New Englanders at my track who walk right out onto the range to pick up balls someone else already has hit—and paid for. It doesn't matter that they are ripping off the club in some small way and putting themselves in grave physical peril as other golfers rain Pinnacles all around them. It's just that they want to do things their way, and save a little money in the process. These, by the way, are the same guys who fill their golf bag pockets with range balls to use on water holes, forgetting all the while that the balls actually belong to someone else.

Most clubs I know have banned cell phones, but I still see people using them all the time. They know they are wrong, but somehow feel that either sheepishness or a tremendous sense of self-importance will save them from any sanction. My favorite scene this past spring was of one of our members talking on his Nokia as he stood by a pay phone near the range, as if the transgression was a little less egregious since there was a legal land phone in the immediate vicinity. The caller looked so guilty and secretive, however, you would have thought he was selling crack rather than checking his messages.

The list goes on and on, from the guy who insists on bringing his dog to the course even though canines have long been banned to the fellow who plays so much golf with his nonmember girlfriend that colleagues have taken to asking jokingly if she had gotten a locker yet. There is also the father-son tandem that sneaks off the 2nd tee to avoid taking a caddie as well as the player who insists on driving his golf cart through the tall fescue like a combine through a corn field, even though there are signs telling him not to.

To those folks, it appears to come down to the same line of thinking: Rules are not only meant to be broken, they are meant to be bent as well.

You don't need no stinking rules when it comes to golf club locker rooms, but those alcoves can present altogether different problems of their own. And in my view those stem from violations of a simple adage I use to gauge the quality of a club by the type of locker room they boast. The more Spartan the locker room, I've found, the better the club and course.

Consider the place at which Jenkins tees it up, an old-line New England retreat with a wonderful golf course and beautiful setting. But the locker room there is very Motel 6.

The big bottle of Scope mouthwash is a nice touch if you want to impress your playing partners with your fresh breath. I am sure the Vitalis hair tonic sitting by the sink has not been used since Tony Lema was toasting his victories with champagne. Ditto the long, black combs soaking in the jar of metallic blue fluid that surely is as toxic as the PCBs lining the bottom of the Hudson River. And while the showers have excellent water pressure, the towels are about the size of bandanas and as soft as sandpaper.

The board of governors at Jenkins's place decided to put air conditioning in the clubhouse a few years ago, but no one ever thought to run a duct or two through the men's locker room, which is located on the ground floor. So on midsummer afternoons, it can be as hot and stifling as a sauna. And the clubhouse staff used the members' locker room to shower and change as well, so Jenkins and his brethren are just as likely to be washing up after a Sunday morning round next to one of their waiters or busboys as they are a fellow member.

Now, some might conclude that that locker room is disgraceful. Or cheap. Or in dire need of improvement. But many of Jenkins's cadres feel it simply says that members care a lot more about the golf than they do on-site personal grooming. If people want to primp and preen, the rationale seems to be, they can do it at their own home. And the New Englander in many of them wonders why they need to be paying for some other member's deodorant. Remember, this is a place where people still play for nickel skins. And a nickel is worth five cents each.

Many of my favorite clubs have much the same attitude. Like the fabled National Golf Links in Long Island. Yes, the main locker room has been redone in the last decade or so, but down the hall from that is the founder's locker room, where the longest-standing members preside. It is a tiny spot that looks like a YMCA, circa 1942, with stand-up metal lockers that clang when they open and shut and are filled with broken hangers. The Naugahyde-lined couches are a nice period touch as well. But the guys there love it because their club is all about golf, and fancy locker-room facilities simply are not that important to them.

That's the same with people at Royal Worlington outside London, who have a marvelous club and a splendid golf course. Their men's locker room has only one shower. So that makes the bet among many foursomes quite easy; the man with the lowest score gets to use the shower first.

I know, golf shrines at Seminole and Pine Valley offer fully loaded locker rooms that fly in the face of my preference. But while they are a definite step above the place where Jenkins tees it up, they don't overdo it. In fact, they do it just right. The towels are big enough to handle even the paunchiest duffer, and all the latest salves and lotions are available. But you never feel as if you are standing in front of a toiletry display counter at Bloomingdale's.

That, however, is not generally the case at newer clubs. They stock their locker rooms as completely as their noontime buffets. You'll find disposable toothbrushes with mint-flavored paste discretely implanted in the bristles. Six different types of facial lotions. Hair mousse and Chanel aftershave. It feels as if you have walked from the course into a Vegas dressing room. And with only a few minutes work, you could look—and smell—like Michael Bolton. Or even Cher.

Some people I know like having all those locker-room treats, but for me, a well-stocked locker room, like a good lunch, doesn't do nearly as much as a good round of golf. Which the places offering that seem to understand.

They also understand the importance of nurturing a homelike atmosphere, which is why one of the toughest things a golfer has to endure each year is the seasonal closing of his club and course. As bad as winter weather gets up north and as depressing as short, cold days often are, nothing is quite so frustrating as your regular retreat being closed. To be sure, you can still get in your rounds during those months. But the games almost always are played at faraway resorts, and no matter how good the layouts, the experience is never really the same.

That's partly because of a lack of familiarity with the courses, and a lack of camaraderie around places that feel as transient as a bus terminal. There are, however, other factors.

Take footwear. One of the pleasures of belonging to a club is having someone take meticulous care of your golf shoes. At my place, cleats are replaced promptly; new laces put in when needed; and leathers shined, polished, and conditioned after each round. Consequently, even the lousiest duffer can look like Beau Brummel when he struts to the 1st tee, his saddles shining in the early morning sun.

But forget about that at most resorts, where golf shoes are the subject of more neglect than a middle child. What that means for the club player is that his FootJoys and Nikes become as ratty as work boots worn by a highway paver. That's why the first thing I do at the start of each golf season is haul in the different shoes I have been wearing all winter to our trusty locker-room attendants, and with a crisp twenty in hand for each, ask if they would please bring them back to life.

Another issue, of course, is my street shoes, none of which would ever get buffed or polished (at least from May through October) if not for those same fellows. Unfortunately, not one of the resorts I ever visit seems to have workers who know how to work with a can of Kiwi black and a good brush.

Cleaning is a problem that can extend to irons and woods as well, and there are few if any of those "pay-to-play-for-a-day" retreats that do quite as good a job in that regard as your own club. I also like the luxury of my bag waiting for me when I get to the pro shop and not having to haul it in and out of my truck, or to and from my room, every time I play.

It also seems that at many resorts, you spend whatever time you are not on the course handing out dollars to whomever is handling your bag as well as to starters, beverage cart drivers, and assorted "valets" and "concierges." After a while, you look and feel like Rodney Dangerfield in *Caddyshack*, peeling ones from a big roll of bills to anyone and everyone who walks by. Back home, it's $5 to the shoe guy every week and whatever I think the caddie deserves in addition to his normal fee.

Actually, there is always something disconcerting about the money a club member has to pay for an individual round of resort golf, and everything else that goes with it. A first-rate course, for example, costs $500 for a day, a price that includes the green fee, a caddie, a snack at the halfway house, a couple of tips and maybe some lunch and a drink afterward. That may only be slightly more than the per-round cost of a golfer paying $7,000 per year in dues for a club at which he plays, say, 25 times a year. But having to cough it up for each 18 you play just seems more expensive. And even if it is comparable financially, it rarely is emotionally, because it is not your place.

There is also the concern of whom you play with. Unless you are foolish enough to sign up for one of those out-of-the-hat scrambles, club golf ensures you go out with people you generally like and enjoy. But visit a resort with anything other than your own foursome, and you are at the mercy of the draw and golf's version of the blind date. Harvey Penick's credo to the contrary, just because someone plays golf does not necessarily make him, or her, your best friend.

Sometimes the frustration and angst that occasionally comes with golf emanates from places away from the club. Consider, for example, this golf shop a good friend of mine owns just down the road from where we regularly tee it up. It is a quiet place where he installs shafts, tweaks lies and lofts, and sells classic books. It also is a spot where people gather to talk about the sport, whether it is a PGA Tour event, Annika Sorenstam's workout regimen, or their own miserable games. I visit the shop once in a while, and its downhome air and breezy gossip remind me of Drucker's Store in *Green Acres*. Only a shaft calibrator replaces the pot-bellied store in this case. And no one is wearing bib overalls.

For years, I found the shop to be a wonderful refuge, and it was easy to get lost in the pleasurable conversations. But I can barely walk through the door any more. It's not that the owner and I have had a falling out, or that my interest in the sport has waned. Rather, I am put off by the emergence of the golf psycho and the way he now dominates so many discussions.

The golf psycho, for the uninitiated, is the person who has become so caught up in the technological minutia that he, or she, can think or talk of nothing else. Forget about appreciating the brilliant design of a Seth Raynor Redan or the views across a stretch of golden fescue as a cock pheasant bursts from the tall grass. The golf psycho is much more interested in the "spining" of his graphite shaft and whether the toe of his 2-iron has been properly grounded.

Now, I am no equipment dinosaur, and my golf bag holds the latest and greatest in woods, irons, and balls. I also know why friends who have scratch handicaps or better get caught up in the subject; they are good enough to truly understand and benefit from subtle changes in their gear and are constantly looking for edges. But it's just not for me, even as my USGA handicap index hovers around 3, and certainly not for those in double digits who could no doubt benefit from having less information spinning around in their heads on the golf course. And I refuse to cross the line by contemplating the optimum length of my driver when I instead could be abusing a player about the sorry state of his game or falling over in laughter at the fellow who splits his khakis when he bends down to mark his ball.

I also have a difficult time hearing others go completely off on the subject, and it makes me sad when I think of how demented they have become. Like the fellow who changed shafts on his driver three times last winter based on how he hit balls at a heated range. Or the guy who walked into the shop to say how the balls he hit with his recently reshafted 3-wood were bouncing "funny" when they landed in the fairway. "Has anyone else here complained about that?" he asked with a straight face. Then there was the 10-handicapper looking for the exact same Nike driver Tiger Woods uses. Estimated price tag: $900. Estimated number of players on this earth who can actually hit a decent shot with that stick: perhaps twelve.

The stories flow steadily out of the shop, and the best ones are often recounted to me. Such as the guy who was getting set to hit balls into a net there a few months ago, so my friend could determine what shafts work best for him.

"What kind of shot do you want me to hit?" the customer asked.

"Just hit some," the storeowner replied.

"You have to tell me what kind of shot you want," he replied. "A butter-cut fade? A honk-and-hook?"

Fortunately for the shopkeeper, the workday was about over, and his partner was already tapping the keg they sometimes set up in back. A lager after that exchange, it seems, was most definitely in order.

Sadly, such madness exists all over the country. A player I know once flew to Arizona for a personal club fitting that cost more than $2,000 and returned home thinking he was ready to tee it up with the pros. Three weeks later, he put a completely different set of custom-made irons in his bag.

I appreciate the passion of these folks, but I do believe they need to ease up. And it wouldn't hurt if they used some of the money they spend on new equipment for a little psychoanalysis.

WHO'S IN CHARGE?

IF YOU WANT a shining example of how not to run a country, consider the African land of Zimbabwe, which is setting new standards for civil ineptitude. And if you are looking for instances of how not to manage a small business, check out your local golf or country club. That's because many of these retreats are so hopelessly inept when it comes to proper administration that it's a shock more don't go belly-up each year.

Now, I do not want to dump unvaryingly on the people who fill the boards and committees at such spots, for they generally are concerned folks who take their roles seriously. But they are often hamstrung by the ineffectual ways most clubs are organized, making them almost impossible to manage.

One major problem is the length of time a president serves at most places. Usually, it's a two-year term, which hardly seems enough time to set forth and then implement a sound agenda. Nor does it allow the person to project any sense of power or longevity, and anyone who wants to seriously buck his initiatives needs only stonewall for a spell before someone else comes along.

Clubs also suffer the same fate as government when it comes to attracting the best and the brightest. Those who sign up frequently have to face the most offensive bickering and second-guessing from self-avowed know-it-alls who have nothing better to do than deride fellow members from the cheap seats. The result is that the most talented people say, "no thanks," when asked to fill a spot, meaning the important positions are often left to second and third choices who can only be regarded as deep-seated masochists with no sense of self-preservation.

How else would I have been chosen to help at my place?

There are exceptions, of course, and some clubs have figured out how to run themselves properly, mostly through benevolent dictators who lead wisely and with great strength. You would think such structures would be emulated throughout the golf world. But the vast majority of clubs in this country seem to assiduously avoid taking steps in that direction. And so does the nation's premier organization for the game, the United States Golf Association (or USGA).

The USGA is a business operation, with approximately $225 million in assets and an annual operating budget of roughly $120 million. Yet it is run much more like a ragtag club than the corporation it should be. Once again, the biggest problem is the management structure. At the head of the USGA is a president who serves two one-year terms. An Executive Committee assembled in mysterious and seemingly arbitrary fashion assists him, as does a shadowy cadre of past USGA presidents who quietly wield considerable influence.

One of the great ironies here is that most of the men in charge at the USGA are members of clubs such as Seminole and Pine Valley that are, in fact, run by omni powerful presidents who are not bound by so-called term limits and never get wobbly in the face of nonsensical member dissent. Clearly, they understand why clubs such as those are so well managed, yet they do not seem the least bit inclined to use those business models for the USGA. Instead, they appear content to follow an exemplar that has made many clubs seem as if the Marx Brothers led them.

That's more than a little surprising, especially given the obvious talents of the people at the USGA. Perhaps no one has made that point better than Jack Vardaman, the association's former general counsel and one-time Executive Committee member, who told the *Washington Post* not so long ago: "The USGA Executive Committee and past presidents have a lot of very smart and successful people, but there is not a single one of them who would run their businesses the way they run the USGA."

Vardaman went on to suggest that the USGA develop a more corporate management structure in an effort to operate like an efficient and prosperous business rather than a club.

That would be a sage thing to do. And golf and country clubs would be wise to follow suit.

The key, of course, is the man or woman on top, and a structure that promotes something of a dictatorial style of leadership.

Now, dictators do not get a lot of respect in the modern world when it comes to running actual countries, and rightfully so. After all, what is there to admire about someone like Robert Mugabe, the megalomaniac who has ruined Zimbabwe? And only time-obsessed train travelers have anything nice to say about Benito Mussolini. In fact, I cannot think of any nation that would be better off in the hands of some iron-fisted autocrat.

Golf clubs, however, are different. They actually thrive under that kind of leadership, and despots who rule with vigor and munificence head the finest ones I know. The head honchos at Augusta National, for example, not only know what is best for their realms but also are unafraid to run them the way they see fit. And they smartly pay little heed to the wants and whims of the people in the streets, in their cases their members.

And they would never do anything so foolish as putting a proposal up for a club vote. My admiration for Thomas Jefferson and James Madison notwithstanding, democracy has no place at a golf club, especially one inhabited by a bunch of accident-by-birth dilettantes who made millions during the easy-money 1990s and suddenly assumed their IQs (and common sense capabilities) were substantially higher than what tests would indicate. Quite simply, most members are not ready for self-government.

Personally, I like the feel of a good golf dictatorship, and it gives me great pleasure to play at a place like that. Maybe it's because I am half-German and prefer order. Or perhaps, I am slowly turning into my father, who ran his household the way Clifford Roberts ran Augusta and once told me after a trip to South Korea that he liked Seoul because it had tanks in the streets at night. It could also be that the most despotic retreats are the only ones that really understand what makes a golf club great, and they seem to do everything right, from having strong caddie programs and heavy-handed bartenders to locker-room attendants who replace the broken Softspikes in your shoes without being asked and remember your name after only one day.

And no one ever, ever steps out of line.

Problem is, these types of places long have been disappearing, and at most clubs today there are too many committees and too much concern over the way all the members think. Few presidents want to anger or embarrass colleagues by disciplining them, no matter how serious the transgression. And if a tough issue comes up, they want to resolve it by vote. Now, democracy may be a fine ideal—and maybe even an imperative—for a political institution, but in golf it only leads to anarchy, with the inmates running the asylum and members believing they can do whatever the hell they want.

Consider the situation at a club I know, where a member decided he did not like the geese that occasionally lolled around the course. In addition to badgering the golf and green chairman about the "problem" for weeks, he took to carrying a pellet gun in his golf bag, and every now and then dusted a honker as it walked by. These assaults, which were illegal under Federal laws governing migratory birds, served mostly to aggravate the Canadas and never drew blood. And in time, they became public knowledge. But it was only after that same member nearly beheaded a goose with his driver in a fit of rage one day that he received a letter of reprimand for his actions. But no punishment was prescribed.

They handle things a bit differently at Pine Valley, where the late John Arthur Brown long served as president. One day, for example, Brown got so exercised at a plodding foursome that he drove out to the course in his golf cart to confront the group. But instead of going up to the golfers themselves, who were standing on the 13th tee, he approached the caddies, who were waiting in the fairway, and said: "That's enough, boys. Pick up those bags and take them back to the clubhouse." And off he drove, leaving the offending players with a rather long walk in and some very strong revelations about proper pace of play.

Another club I visit fairly often employs a similar disdain for inappropriate behavior, and members there delight in telling the tale of a woman who inexcusably berated a dining room worker during a post-golf lunch. Word of the transgression quickly made its way to the president of the club, who promptly called the offender at home.

The president knew that she and her husband lived 20 minutes away from the club, and he gave her exactly half an hour to return and apologize to the server as well as the general manager, or her locker would be cleaned out and her membership summarily terminated. He also mentioned that her husband would get tossed as well.

Needless to say, the couple appeared at the club entrance within 25 minutes, slightly screeching their car to a halt in the gravel driveway before rushing to offer regrets to anyone who would listen and genuflecting in front of the president as if he were royalty.

Of course, the most famous club dictator of all time was Clifford Roberts of Augusta National, and the best-known demonstration of his leadership philosophy involved a pine tree off the left side of the 17th fairway of that hallowed course. Roberts was presiding over a board of governors meeting in 1956, and Dwight

Eisenhower, who happened to be our nation's President at the time, suggested the club cut down the tree. Roberts immediately ruled Augusta's most prestigious member out-of-order and then adjourned the meeting. And the pine stayed just where it was.

Another of the great golf dictators was Mrs. Joseph V. Reed of the Jupiter Island Club in Hobe Sound, Florida. Mrs. Reed's family owned the land on which the club was built, and she ruled it like an impatient empress. One of her tactics was to have people photographed in the act of committing obvious and egregious infractions, such as wearing golf shorts that were too short, and then sent them a letter of admonishment. If you got more than a letter or two from her, it was probably time to move off the island.

Jupiter Island members feared Mrs. Reed more than the taxman and would submit to almost any embarrassment to avoid getting on her bad side. Like the friend of mine who was putting on the 18th green one winter afternoon when one of Mrs. Reed's small dogs wrapped himself around the golfer's leg in what can only be described as an amorous embrace. The man tried to shed the overfriendly canine by fiercely shaking his leg, but froze instantly when Mrs. Reed called out from her nearby cart: "Stop kicking my dog!" And so he just stood there until one of her aides pulled the mutt away.

It has often been averred that the man or woman running the golf or country club has the toughest job in town. But as far as I am concerned, it actually is the person who heads the club's golf committee, for his realm is often as hopelessly chaotic as the streets of Paris during the French Revolution.

As a rule, the golf chairman is in charge of a club's golf programs and oversees all that goes on in that department, from hiring the professional to scheduling tournaments. But that is not all the golf chairman does. He also has to battle those boorish members who believe they not only know everything about the game (even though they have played for less than five years), but feel it is their right if not their bounded duty to scrutinize and critique whatever goes on, no matter how reckless or ill-mannered their commentaries might be.

He makes policy, enforces rules, disciplines deviants, runs meetings, and settles disputes. He takes calls at all hours and submits to constant buttonholing and haranguing wherever he may go. I have seen golf chairmen cornered at funerals and accosted in grocery stores, with one member complaining that the rough is too long five minutes after another has insisted it is too short. And I have even heard of some committee heads being physically threatened.

Like my friend Jenkins, who found an unsigned note hanging ominously in his locker one afternoon. It read: "Get rid of the geese, or we will get rid of you."

And his is supposed to be a nice family club.

Unfortunately, those sorts of things happen to golf chairman all the time. Jenkins knows this firsthand, as he held that position at his club for a while, and the nonsense started the day he accepted the position. That's when he found one of his older members hitting balls at the practice range right next to a sign indicating the facility was off limits because of wet weather. After watching the man take five divots the size of beaver pelts and remove most of the turf from that section of the tee, he approached him and said: "I'm sorry, sir, but the range is closed." The member didn't even look up as he replied: "Not for me, it ain't."

Sometimes the abuse can last a whole morning, as it did for Jenkins some years ago when he tried to qualify for the top flight of his club championship. He had just hit his drive on the first hole and was walking to his ball when the pro called him back to the tee to settle a dispute with one of the club's more contentious members. It seems he did not want to play in the threesome to which he had been assigned, even though that was the rule, and Jenkins had to haggle with him for nearly 15 minutes before the malcontent finally relented. And then he felt so good about the confrontation that he went on to top his second shot and finished No. 1 with a bogey 6.

He did manage to right himself on the 2nd hole and was enjoying a pretty good round when one of the men playing in that following group became so enraged at the aforementioned fellow's incessantly bad behavior that he quit his round and decided to walk off. However, he felt it his duty to tell Jenkins all about it before he left the course, jawing his every complaint as they walked to the 9th green. Needless to say, my friend was so heartened by the exchange, and the Roller Derby-like tension in the group behind him that he proceeded to 3-putt.

But the real topper came on the last hole, as Jenkins was putting for a medal score that was surely going to be too high to qualify. Just as he brought his club back, a ball landed on the green and closely skipped by. You guessed it, the member he had been arguing with on No. 1 had just hit into him.

Jenkins thought for a moment after going after the knucklehead with his 4-iron, but instead simply picked up his ball and went home for the rest of the day. And he did not return for two weeks, so furious was he over what had happened that morning, and so tired of having to play proctor for a golf program that seemed to have become a sporting cross between *Romper Room* and the *Jerry Springer Show*.

I remember thinking at the time that no other committee chairman had ever suffered such indignities, but then I heard about a gentleman at another club who had grown so frustrated at the way he was harassed at his home course during his reign as golf chairman that he stopped playing there on weekends and instead went to another club on those days to hit balls.

Some people, it seems, will do almost anything to get away from the job.

There is a tendency at times for clubs to deal with such problems through the promulgation of rules, or at the very least the enforcement of laws already on the books. I even know of one place when things got so bad that the Board convened a sort of retreat to determine whether they should clamp down on discipline and begin enforcing the rules of their club again, or simply forget about it all and let the mobs continue to run the streets. Now, it pains me even to think that such a conclave was necessary, or that there was even a doubt as to what action to take. But at least the club leaders eventually came to their senses and decided to take charge again, no matter what it would take.

The subject of rules is not a complicated one for me, however, and I long ago determined that the only one a club ever needs to concern itself with comes not from something the USGA published but rather the Book of Matthew in the Bible, chapter 7, verse 12.

That's the one that goes: "Therefore all things whatsoever ye would that men should do to you, do even so to them . . ."

It's better known as the Golden Rule, and the premise of "doing unto others as you would have them do unto you" not only is found in scriptures of nearly every religion in the world, but is regarded as a moral compass for right living. Especially on the golf course.

I came to that conclusion after listening to my friend Jenkins decry the different efforts at his place to get people there to behave themselves better. Mostly, it entails the exhausting formulation of standards governing everything from cell phone usage to proper attire, and it has served to make the yearbook at his club as voluminous as the IRS tax code—and just as tedious and confusing to read. It has also caused him to wonder about the sensibility of issuing directives as rapidly as the U.S. Congress and what it says about the direction his retreat is taking.

His understandable concern is that it is becoming a club of rules, and every time a member slips in the slightest, the reaction is to put a new law in the books. That's bad management, in my opinion, and his place would be far better off if it simply threw away all those regulations and focused club philosophy on that one Bible verse I first heard as a young man in Sunday School.

Do unto others, indeed.

If golfers acted that way, they would bring an Eden-like calm and conviviality to their clubs. They would replace every divot, repair every pitch mark, and rake every bunker. They would pick up their broken tees after hitting their drives and dispose of them properly. They would play with a comfortable sense of urgency, never tarrying long enough to hold up other players or take more than four hours to complete a round. They would dress properly, saving their short shorts and gruesome mock T's for other endeavors, and understand they should always remove their hats and visors when they walk inside.

They always would consider how their actions affected others as opposed to thinking only of themselves. Which means, ideally, that they wouldn't dare bring their cell phones out of their cars or pound the keys of their BlackBerrys as they wait for their drinks at the 19th hole. They would play only with their fellow members at peak times and strive to bring their guests during slack periods of play, so as not to inconvenience the club. They would take caddies whenever possible, buy all their balls and clothes from their PGA professionals, treat their club staffs with respect and understanding, and tip the guys in the locker room who shine their shoes as well as the fellows who serve drinks and snacks in the hallway house. And they would yell "Fore!" when they hit an errant shot but otherwise do their best not to be heard outside their own foursome.

They would, in summary, act like ladies and gentlemen when they go to their clubs, and there would never be a reason to print reams and reams of regulations—only the need to abide by that simple verse in Matthew.

Philosophers have pondered the meaning of the Golden Rule for years and advanced various interpretations. Among the most thoughtful modern thinkers on the subject is Harry J. Gensler, a professor at John Carroll University in Cleveland as well as the author of books on morals and ethics. He opines: "to apply the Golden Rule adequately, we need knowledge and imagination. We need to know what effect our actions have on the lives of others. And we need to be able to imagine ourselves, vividly and accurately, in the other person's place. . . ."

"The Golden Rule is best seen as a consistency principle. . . . It prescribes consistency (and) it tests our moral coherence. If we violate the Golden Rule, then we're violating the spirit of fairness and concern that lies at the heart of morality."

I read those passages to Jenkins and asked him simply: What else do we as golfers truly need to know?

ADMISSION
ADMONITIONS

SOME FRIENDS of mine argue that the most important committee of any club is the one that oversees the golf program. Others believe is the group that handles maintenance and operation of the course, or those who take care of finances. But I have to cast my vote for the cabal that runs membership.

Why?

Because no layout is worth playing if it is populated by people so rebarbative and ill-mannered they couldn't get on the waiting list of Bushwood if Dr. Beeper was their father. And it is never easy keeping those barbarians at the gate.

My sense is that the very best clubs in the land are those with the most stringent admissions policies and most inclined to follow an "invitation only" format, where powers-that-be scrutinize potential members and offer places in their sanctums only after a lengthy and, ahem, discreet vetting. There are no waiting lists, no specious testimonials from so-called supporters and no cocktail party crawls, where candidates are socially poked and prodded like cattle at a livestock auction. That is not only a demeaning process to all involved but also wildly inefficient, as prodigious amounts of alcohol are usually served during those beauty pageants, resulting in the sort of clouded judgment that over-served college seniors use ten minutes before closing time. And anyone, even an ax murderer, can behave himself for a few fetes.

The folks who take care of admissions at my place do a pretty good job (forgetting for a moment that they were the same ones who let me in). But that hasn't stopped my friend Jenkins from coming up with ways to improve the process. Or, at the very least, make it more interesting.

For starters, you should be able to throw out an old member for every new one you let in. Not only would that induce people to make only judicious sponsorships (knowing that their cherished spots could be threatened by anyone who comes aboard), but it also would give clubs an annual escape clause, a sort of membership mulligan if you will, where folks who once seemed like good additions could quickly and quietly be put back where they belong, which, of course, is out on the street.

Secondly, club employees should get to toss out one member per year. They deal with people around there more regularly and know the cool guys from the jerks.

Plus, you have to figure the members they most likely would target for expulsion would be those who treat them badly, and nothing is quite so egregious in any club situation than mistreatment of the staff. Serves them right, then, to suffer.

Another thought is auctioning off one membership per year to the highest bidder. For a lot of exclusive, old-line clubs in big-income areas, that would solve their financial problems on an annual basis as big-monied high rollers would fall all over themselves to spend $10,000 for one of those precious slots. And if the people who cough up the most dough turn out to be complete dolts, the club leadership needs only to ask the staff to vote them off the island the following year.

While we are on the subject of money, why not a system where new members have to pay only what they can afford? Use a percentage of net worth or annual income instead of a set initiation fee, and a corporate bigwig with a Warren Buffett-like bank account, for example, would be liable for a much larger amount than, say, a semi-impoverished golf writer.

Call me comrade, but that seems fair to me.

In looking at club membership problems, it is also important to address the issue of sponsors, as I have often found those who put up people barely know the candidates' names. Instead, they are doing a friend a favor, furthering a business relationship, or desperately trying to appease an insistent spouse. And though the intent may be innocuous, the result frequently is not, and all the club really does is add one more knuckle-head to the rolls.

So, here's how to handle that problem: Any sponsor proposing a candidate who ultimately gets turned down gets thrown out of the club. Also, if your guy ever gets into trouble and needs to be disciplined, you as the sponsor have to face a comparable penalty. But only after you have chastised the blowhard you helped get in, as it is always best that the person in charge of that candidate remain the one responsible for him through-out the life of his association with the club—and the one who is first responder should he ever step out of line. After all, why should club leaders have to baby-sit your great idea?

And a person who does not play golf should not be allowed to put up a candidate who does. The thought being, why should the rest of the membership get stuck with a fellow the proposer will never have to play with? And how well can he possibly know a candidate if they have never teed it up together?

Jenkins and I were remarking the other day about how much things have changed at many clubs the past couple decades in that it used to be all about the golf experience at the very best places. But now, it is all about getting in. I think it is safe to say that getting in has cer-tainly become more difficult—and in many cases more desperate—for prospective members of the sorts of high-quality clubs that dominate *Golfweek*'s Top 100 roster of classic courses. There are endless waiting lists, intense letter-writing campaigns, and intolerable social outings. And where's the merit in a process that usually demands intense scrutiny by admission committees populated with members so emotionally inept and frightfully devoid of good judgment when it comes to personality and character they'd be the first folks you'd want to throw out once you joined?

It's gotten so bad in some locales that a favorite pastime of prospective members is watching for the flag behind the clubhouse to be lowered to half-mast, indicating a current member has died—and a space has likely opened up. A tough flu season may be considered a tragedy in most minds. But to the person trying to claw his or her way into a hot club—and looking for room on the rolls—a light thinning of the senior membership is not necessarily a bad thing and has been known to cause a crush of calls for information on head count.

"I belong to a place where it now takes a non-legacy nearly 30 years to receive full golf privileges," says Jenkins. And to illustrate his point, he recalls an elderly widow he met during a recent new member cocktail party. "She was nearly in her 80s and having just gotten in said to me, 'It's too bad Harry didn't live to see this.'" Harry, you see, was her late husband. And he had had the misfortune to die on the waiting list.

It didn't always used to be that way. As recently as the mid-70s, it was possible to join one of the country's great clubs without a whole lot of hassle so long as you had a keen passion for the game and demonstrated an ability to get along with members and behave yourself on the course. Excessive net worth didn't hurt, but it was not a determining factor. And neither was a lineage that could be traced back to the Mayflower.

But private clubs of almost all levels today can in some cases be as tough to crack as a bank vault. And people seem willing to do—and endure—almost anything to get in.

Like this man not far from where I live who so badly wanted to join the golf club bordering his house that he agreed to sell it a sliver of land on which a small parking lot would be built for a song. The deal was sealed, the lot constructed and the neighbor sure it would be only a matter of time before his application was approved (and his generosity duly rewarded). But when it came to a vote before the Board of Governors, they unceremoniously turned the man down. The club, it seemed, had decided that while it wanted the land, it did not want him.

I know another guy who figured the best way to advance his candidacy for a different place was to throw a party for himself and invite some 200 members. That seemed a little aggressive to some. But their dismay over that was nothing compared to the outrage that occurred after the man, who happened to be a well-known business mogul, told a national newspaper reporter he could get into any club in America. "Not this one," was the way most Board members felt after that comment appeared. And they became even more committed to that sentiment a few weeks later when the person was accused of chasing his neighbor across his lawn in a drunken rage, all the while pelting the neighbor's Lily Pulitzer sundress with fireballs from a Roman candle.

This was a person, by the way, who was a member of the coveted club. And it was she who suggested to the Board the following day that the man's membership application be, shall we say, withdrawn.

But many applications make it through each year, and it is always fun to watch how new members' behavior changes once they really don't have to behave anymore. A friend who served for many years as admissions chairman at his place remembers how prospective members would stop talking to him after they joined. "The act was over, and as soon as they didn't need me any more, they treated me like an ex-spouse," he says. "And I usually didn't hear from them again until they wanted to get one of their kids in, or maybe one of their friends."

That same friend also speaks to the inevitable occurrence that came with his appointment to that post. "I get named admissions chairman, and suddenly I am the hit of the social circuit, and everybody, and I mean everybody, put me on their guest list," he recalls. "Mostly, I would stand in a corner of a room, and people would be lined up to speak with me as if I was in a receiving line, and I swear some of them wanted to kiss my ring. As soon as my term was over, though, I was put back in Siberia."

Another problem, of course, is the new member who immediately sets out to express his opinion, assuming that paying his initiation has given him carte blanche to say anything he wants about the club, and offer his view on everything from green speed and tournament formats to the layout of the locker room and the texture of the sand in the bunkers. That sort of behavior irks Jenkins so much that he has come up with a special rule for newcomers: They should not show up for the first year of membership, and then should not open their mouth for the next four.

He has also concocted a guideline he feels all admissions chairmen should assiduously follow: The more club memberships a candidate already has to his credit, the more likely he will be an exemplary addition to his. Part of that is a result of experience and exposure, and also because no bad actor can possibly pass muster with more than a couple of admissions committees in a lifetime before being ousted. In addition, a golfer with a quiver full of clubs is usually a successful and financially secure soul, so well grounded in terms of personality and ego that he does not need to act out the way someone of, say, slightly less stature and verve does. On the other hand, those with only one or two memberships to their names sometimes carry themselves as if they still have something to prove.

Over the years, Jenkins has come to the conclusion that the very best private clubs are not only the hardest to get into but also the least expensive. That's the case with places like Pine Valley and Augusta, where dues and initiation fees are as modest as their barriers to entry are high.

Ironically, many of the newer—and perhaps less traditional—clubs that are much more costly to join can be much more difficult to leave than to get in, as members there have to find someone to take their place so they can recoup their initiation money. In actuality, there are waiting lists to leave, and no number of sudden deaths is going to speed up the process.

But as bad as that may be for some club members, they can always comfort themselves by the fact that while they may be waiting to get out, they were at the very least able to get in.

Of course, getting in takes on very different connotations when divorce is somehow involved and couples are fighting over their spots in a club as intensely as they are haggling about their possession of their houses and cars. What that usually means is admissions committees have to determine who actually holds memberships and who has to reapply if he, or she, wants back in.

I know several clubs where the rule on this issue is quite straightforward, and Jenkins would have no doubt been pleased to be associated with one of those places as a matter of simplicity and clarity. Why? Because the man always is the member, and he kept the status in the event of a divorce. If his soon-to-be ex-wife wanted to stay on as well, she has to apply as a new member.

Now, that bit of dinosaur logic has long ago changed at most clubs, including the place where Jenkins plays his golf. There, it is the legacy, or the one person who has been a member the longest, who automatically keeps the bond, gender be damned, while the Johnny-come-lately is the one who has to grovel for a new opening of his, or her, own.

Experience tells me the diviners of such sensible policy like to attribute their actions to heartfelt pangs of fairness and feminism, and that may be so in some cases. But more often than not, I believe, these modifications were actually born of some very bad experiences in which low-rent spouses of distaff legacies retained their memberships even as their true colors, and increasingly obvious character flaws, were revealed in one police blotter incident after another.

That's what happened at Jenkins's club, and the impetus for the rule change there is famously attributed to a situation involving a member's daughter and her misanthropic spouse, who possessed all the class of a sideshow hawker yet received the much-coveted membership when the union crumbled. Not only did that transaction cause a collective groan among an exasperated membership and instigate an emergency meeting of the Board, in which the club constitution was altered, but it also prompted the father of the legacy to reflect on her initial meeting with that twit as a college student and ask: "Don't you think you could have moved down one bar stool?"

The issue of rogue spouses has become of such concern at some clubs that Jenkins wonders whether admissions committee members should become part of the actual prenuptial counseling, sitting alongside parish priests as they interview happy couples and advising as to the likelihood of their marriages working at the club as well as in the home.

Not everyone is as concerned about the people with whom legacies are hooking up, however. In fact, one fellow I know actually is approaching his daughter's recent admission as a junior member to their club, as well as her purchase of a condominium, as a sort of dowry situation and is hoping they will soon find some eligible guy attracted not only by his child's striking looks and stunning intellect but also by her ready-made membership in a top club. To him, it has only increased her chances in marriage as well as the possibility of her being able to afford the onerous initiation fee (and rely a bit less on Mom and Dad's VISA card). And not to worry if there is trouble in paradise down the road: The by-laws at that place state that as the legacy, she gets to keep the membership.

Legacies are often interesting studies because at many clubs, the overriding sense is that they would have never gotten in if their parents had not been members. That is certainly the case with me at my place, and ditto for several of my best golfing buddies, there and at other spots. But it bothers us not one bit. In fact, we laugh at the near certainty of our rejections if we actually had to have come in off the streets, and we do the same about the guys who married daughters of longtime members, or, in the words of Jenkins, got rich in church. They are part of what we call the First Wives Club.

Inherent in the conundrum of divorce is the issue of remarriage. At one place I frequent, anyone who decides to stroll down the aisle again technically has to reapply for membership as well, the thinking being that his or her new spouse should have to make the grade with admissions before hanging around the pool. On the surface, that seems a reasonable procedure. But the practice has gone a long way toward stifling whatever matrimonial urges have risen up in several single friends of mine looking to rise up from the ashes of divorce with a new life partner. And they are loathe to give their clubs any opportunity to reconsider their own

candidacies and correct the obviously egregious mis-
takes the clubs made by letting them in to begin with.
It's called marrying out of your club, and one golf
friend actually waited until he became president of his
place before putting a ring on his finger again, so concerned he was of that happening to him.

And you thought lawyers and judges were the
toughest part of divorce.

BACK IN THE LOOP
(AND SOMETIMES
THROWN FOR ONE)

IT WAS IN a bar one night last summer that I found the elixir for golf's participation problems, and the difficulty in bringing young people into the game. And it came in the form of a couple of college graduates who insisted on buying me a drink

I actually knew both fellows, for they were long-time caddies at the club to which I belong. They had spent several seasons lugging bags across our course—reading putts, walking off yardages, and coddling golfers of all ages and abilities. They had even received modest educational stipends from a scholarship we had started to help them through college. Now, they were off in the business world, one toiling for a New York investment bank and the other running a lucrative chiropractic practice.

Maybe it was the Patron Silver we were drinking together, so welcoming on a brisk winter's eve. Or perhaps it was the worries I had heard expressed in recent years throughout the golf industry, and the concerns everyone from club makers to course owners shared about people who were either shunning the game or leaving it altogether. But half an hour into my session with the former loopers, I suddenly hit upon a workable solution to the issues of participation, one that not only seemed sensible but also was devoid of politics and the sort of theoretical altruism that causes realists to gnash their teeth.

It was about caddies and once again making them a significant part of the golfing landscape.

Consider these two fellows. They had started caddying in their early teens, and not only enjoyed summer employment for the better part of a decade but also learned how to play (thanks primarily to open caddie play on Mondays). They became quick studies on rules and etiquette (mostly because of caddie clinics they regularly attended and simple observation during dozens of rounds). And when they were finally ready to leave college, as well as the club membership they had served for so long, they had all the necessary credentials to become contributing members of our golfing society. They carried middle-range handicaps. They understood such essentials as keeping a good pace of play and faithfully repairing every divot and pitch mark. They felt comfortable in and around pro shops and confidentially played wherever they traveled. They could also rib, kibitz, harangue, and deride their opponents and playing partners with Trevino-like prowess.

In other words, they were everything the powers of golf want to produce, players with the financial and emotional wherewithal to tee it up twenty or thirty times a year.

How did they get that way?

Not by building a handful of executive courses in high-need areas, or, as one misguided speaker at a golf participation conference once suggested, by repainting a Pinehurst pub so it appeared brighter and more hospitable to distaff golfers.

No, they got that way by caddying. And nothing is able to educate so many potential golfers, and entice them not only to start playing a true sport for life but also remain a part of it for decades, than that vocation.

Problem is, caddie programs have disappeared as quickly as persimmons.

A number of America's top golf clubs and resorts have these programs, but they employ mostly pro jocks who are already part of the golf world. Sadly, most of those spots have little or no time for loopers of high school or college age, and that also appears to be the case with the types of golf and country clubs that used to utilize scads of local youths but became addicted over the years to the easy revenues of golf cart fleets. A lot of these facilities just got lazy and quit enforcing rules deeming that caddies be used at certain times. Or they stopped employing caddie masters and running the kinds of clinics that made the youngsters proficient loopers. They also forgot about explaining to their memberships the benefits of putting resident teens to work, not only as a way of giving back to the community and uniting the club behind a common cause but also in getting to know a handful of young people and participating in some small way in their maturation.

The result is that perhaps the best pipeline into the game was more or less shut down, one that cost next to nothing to run but paid huge dividends for all involved. All it really required was an emotional commitment, a supervisor to keep the caddie pen running smoothly and an understanding of what caddies mean to golf.

The industry powers that fret about the problems of participation would be wise to consider a nationwide program that addresses the caddie issue and gets clubs back in the loop. Chances are, it will work better than anything else they have tried.

Who knows, an old caddie may even want to buy them a drink one day.

My advocacy for caddies goes back many years, and that is not only because they occasionally sate my lust for adult beverages. However, I am not always in the majority as far as that goes. In fact, I have encountered almost as much resistance to caddies in my time as I have support. Some golfers don't like to be told what to do, especially those New Englanders in my part of the world who pride themselves on fierce independence. Yankees also have a tendency to please to the point of obsessiveness with their frugality, and they are loath to spend a dime on anything unless they absolutely have to.

Yes, price can be a problem, and, say, $50 a bag is a lot of money for any golfer. (As a journalist who long ago took a vow of poverty to ply my passion, I can well understand that attitude.) But there are so many things that players get from that investment beyond someone who simply lugs around their Ogios and cleans off their clubs. They also receive companionship on the course from someone with whom they can share the good moments in a round and get help making their ways through the bad. At places such as mine, it also means assisting a young man looking to earn some money in the summer, which immediately makes me think back to all those summers my friends and I worked around our home town, whether mowing lawns or cleaning swimming pools or painting houses. Those jobs were important, and so were the people who hired us, whether by the hour, day, or week. They not only filled our wallets with money but also our heads with lessons of life.

Not surprisingly, my favorite caddies are those that carry at my place. They are a distinct and personable bunch, the vast majority in high school and college, and I've known many of them since they first showed up to loop in their very early teens. But I also enjoy taking caddies at other clubs I visit, as I delight in learning the lore of those places and getting a feel for those areas. Many times, a good caddie is like a good docent, especially as you work your way around a historic track and soak up all it has to offer.

One of the most common complaints at clubs like mine that mostly employ younger caddies is that the kids are lost out on the course their first couple seasons, wandering around in dazes as they try to grasp all the nuances of the craft. Now, I appreciate that can be difficult for some. But I always enjoy going out with those lads, doing what I can to help them along as I attempt to learn a little bit more about who they are and what they are all about. In fact, I almost always prefer those kids to the older caddies I so often encounter at the better clubs and courses in this land. To be sure, many of those veterans are first-rate loopers with excellent playing skills, years of experience, keen green-reading skills, and the sort of soothing personality that can nurture a 76 out of even the most troubled player.

But they can also present their own set of problems, and ones that are far greater than those of a 13-year-old who doesn't quite know where to stand for a shot.

One comes in the form of the caddie who feels compelled to offer on-course—and quite unsolicited—golf lessons. Few things get my goat more quickly than a fellow telling me I need to grip my 6-iron differently or suggesting that I fiddle with my swing, especially when I have not asked for their help and we have been together for only a few holes. After thirty years of playing the game, I more or less know what I am doing wrong when my game goes South. And if I concentrate hard enough, I can usually find a way to fix it. Occasionally, I will ask a caddie if I am moving my head on putts, or coming off the ball on my drives, and I always appreciate the assistance. But only when it comes from my initiation.

Another thing that irks me is the way some of the older, more experienced caddies try to club my every shot after only a hole or two. Occasionally, I am able to gel with the guy on my bag as he demonstrates a sudden and innate understanding of my game and what I am capable of. But more times than not, a caddie seeing me for the first time has about as much knowledge of what I can do on the course as I have of molecular biology. So, all I want on those occasions is the yardage. I know how I am swinging. I know how I have been playing. Just give me a distance and let me worry about the club I use for that.

Those types of loopers are also prone to forgetting that the course and club—and not the person on the bag—is the "show" and the reason you have traveled to a certain retreat. For far too many caddies, the fairways are a sort of comedy club stage, and that means I get guys trying to be Jerry Seinfeld instead of Fluff Cowan. Either they are telling me jokes between shots, recounting their sexual exploits from the night before, or rambling on about the significance of the Stinger tee and why it works for them. I've even had caddies pull out samples of their poetry that they have read on our way down the fairway, and my only thought is that if I wanted that as part of my recreational routine, I would move to Greenwich Village and nose around for "open mike" nights.

However, nothing is more bothersome than the caddie that feels the need to "switch up" my golf bag. And I still remember the first time that happened to me. I was in Pebble Beach, getting ready to play the wonderful Golf Links for the first time on a beautiful April morning and feeling like I was in sports heaven. Then, my Nazi caddie appeared. He looked innocent enough, I thought at first glance, dressed in a looper's jumpsuit and smiling heartily. But in his hand was an empty Pebble Beach carry bag, and as soon as he set it down, he started transferring clubs from my bag to his.

"What are you doing?" I asked, and it was a legitimate question. For one thing, I had a carry bag of my own that could not have possibly weighed more than his. And as a matter of consideration on this sunny day, I had left my rain suit and umbrella in the car. So, all I had was fourteen clubs, maybe a dozen balls, some tees and markers, a tube of sun block, and a reporter's notebook and a couple of pens. In other words, mine was not exactly a Rodney Dangerfield situation, with a golf bag the size of a late-model Cadillac and a sound system a Deadhead would be proud to call his own.

"We do this all the time because it is easier on us," my caddie said, without the slightest hint of a German accent. "You can't believe the bags people want us to carry."

"There's nothing wrong with my bag," I said indignantly. "It has practically nothing in it, the legs work fine and the strap is brand new. Plus, I may need something from it during the round. So please, just leave the clubs where they are."

My caddie looked at me sharply, and when he saw that I wasn't going to budge (and realized he had no legitimate argument), he acquiesced, slinging my bag over his shoulder and heading out to the first tee.

As it turned out, we had a nice round together. But I hated what had happened that morning. For one thing, it is a lousy way to start what promised to be a good golf day, especially over such a trivial matter.

If I wanted conflict like that, I reasoned, I always could call my ex-wife, or one of my editors.

Then, there is the issue of who was working for whom. Now, I was not looking to assert my power as the customer, and I would never, ever treat anyone who provides a service as anything other than an equal. But it defies logic to have a person who is paid roughly $100 for five hours of work, which is among the highest rates in the game, tell me whether I could use my own bag. Especially after I also have paid $350 in green fees. If we were talking about conforming to a dress code, I would understand. Ditto, if it were a question of wearing spikeless shoes or playing at a certain pace of play. But a golf bag that might not make a weight limit?

That experience at Pebble was a first for me, so I thought it was just an aberration. But when I went to Spyglass the following day, it happened again. This time, my caddie did not relent so easily, and we debated heatedly outside the pro shop before he determined that carrying my bag would not do him any physical harm or cause him to work harder than he really wanted.

I tried to put the incident behind me as we strolled down the first hole, and after my third shot stopped 20 feet from the pin, I felt I had. My caddie read my birdie putt, and I followed his advice. But what he predicted would break right actually broke hard left, and I ended up three-jacking.

Four times over the next five holes he gave me incorrect distances or bad reads, and I first thought he was simply horrible at what he did, which can be another problem with caddies at big-time tracks who think and act like they know a lot more about golf and the course than they really do. Or maybe he was just paying me back for our little tiff. I figured it had to be the latter, and I remembered doing the same thing to customers when I waited tables years ago; if someone gave me a hard time for no apparent reason, their soup took an extra 15 minutes to arrive.

By the time we reached the turn, I had given up on my caddie all together and figured all the yardages and reads myself. Nothing like traveling 3,000 miles and paying several hundred dollars for a little passive aggression.

I was afraid the madness would continue the following day at Cypress Point when my assigned caddie came out to greet me with a club carry bag. I quickly said we were taking my bag, even if I had to carry it myself and pay him to walk along. "Whatever you like," he said with a smile as he put down the club bag. "You're the boss."

It was nice to be back on friendly ground.

FOR THE LOVE
OF LOGOS

CERTAIN PEOPLE might argue that the biggest developments in golf the past decade or so have been the enormous advances in technology. But I think first prize should go to the growing prominence—and perceived importance—of golf and country club logos.

It used to be that the designs you saw on most golf shirts or sweaters represented a major apparel or equipment maker. But now, club logos are all the rage. And where there once was a Munsingwear penguin or Lacoste crocodile is now a Seminole Indian or Myopia fox head.

One reason for this phenomenon is looks. As a rule, club logos are infinitely more attractive than anything designed on Seventh Avenue or produced in a Central American sweatshop. The best ones are simple in design, small in size, and historic in nature. They also evoke a clear sense of the club's image. Such as the Fisher's Island island, which to the eye of the uninitiated might actually appear to be a bit of abstract art. But to those that know golf, it stands as a symbol of excellence and class.

I think people also like the connection to golf the club logo represents. I mean, what does Ralph Lauren and his little polo player really have to do with the sport? But someone who enjoys good golf—and a good golf experience—can relate much more easily to the wicker basket on Merion's shirt than to the name of the person who used to dress Brooke Shields in blue jeans.

But the biggest reason for this rush to logos is status. A shirt from Cypress Pint or Prairie Dunes says more than anything a golfer can get at Bloomingdale's or Saks.

It's also a matter of country clubs in general—and good ones in particular—becoming so much harder to get into. When someone makes the cut these days, they usually want to share the accomplishment with the world, and one way to do that is to plaster the club logo on everything they own. It's another sign, along with the BMW, the nanny, the plasma television, and the Labrador Retriever, that they have arrived.

"I think the logo has almost gotten bigger, in some cases, than the membership itself," says my friend Jenkins. "When people get into my club, they cannot wait to put the little windshield sticker with the club logo on their cars. That not only tells the guard at the security gate that they are members, but also the entire town. And people notice."

The thing is, that status-enhancing sticker can sometimes lead to scorn.

"My wife determined some years ago that we didn't need to advertise our membership, so we never put any stickers on our car," Jenkins recalls. "I wasn't sure I agreed with the practice until the day I went to a local car wash, and the woman in front of me, who happened to be a member of my club and have a sticker on her vehicle, pulled away after an argument with one of the workers. 'What a stuck-up bitch,' the man shouted as she drove off. 'All those country club people are alike.'"

Displaying the logo of your club is one thing, but flying the colors of one you are not a member of—and probably could not get into even if you were a legacy— is another matter. Some might describe it as blatant wannabe-ism, and there is an element of truth to that. But it is also the case of a Shinnecock Hills or Chicago Golf simply having an enviably attractive logo as well as a wonderful—and well-deserved—reputation as a great place to play. That's why many of my golf shirts and sweaters come from places like that. No foul there, as far as I am concerned. But it can present its own set of problems.

Like the time when I was having lunch at Cypress Point. I had just dipped into my Minestrone when one of my playing partners said, "Well, I guess you have had quite a winter at your club." I had no idea what he was talking about until I remembered I was wearing a Seminole wind vest (and there had been a recent change in leadership at that Florida retreat). You see, my lunch companion assumed, as most members of his generation would, that a person only wore the logo of a club to which he belonged. Much chagrined, I muttered something about it being quite a winter indeed, and stared hard into my soup bowl, hoping the conversation subject would quickly change.

Interestingly, the recent fascination with club logos has prompted many clubs to sell two types of apparel—one that has only the logo (for members), and another, for guests, that has both the logo and the club name. It's a great way of separating the "Select" from "Great Unwashed Who Somehow Managed to Get through the Gates."

My friend Jenkins found out about that during a visit to Royal St. George's in England. He was wandering through the pro shop when he spied a lovely, charcoal gray, cashmere sweater with the club logo, an image of old St. George charging forth on his mount.

"Excellent choice," said the pro as Jenkins put it down on the counter. "But I am afraid it is not for you.

Then, he directed him to the "other" part of the shop.

Not too long after that humbling retort, Jenkins joined me and a handful of colleagues who are among the men and women who rate the layouts that make up *Golfweek*'s annual America's Best list of classic and modern courses. Our venue for this gathering was a top private club, and we were supposed to be discussing architecture and the various layouts we had visited—and assessed—in the past months. But the conversation soon turned to the matter of club logos. That's because as our fellow appraisers walked by our breakfast table that morning, we noticed each one wore a shirt, windbreaker or sweater—or some combination thereof—emblazoned with icons and initials from some of the finest retreats in the land. Several sported the Pine Valley shield, for example, or the Augusta flag. I also spied the Maidstone whale, the Ocean Forest tree and wave and the Kittansett seashell. And it did not take my friends and I long to determine there was a strong protocol as to how this savvy bunch of golfers wore their logos, and even which ones they displayed on a given day.

The first thing I discerned was that everyone had carefully mixed his or her batch of trademarks. By that, I mean no one appeared fully bedecked in one club logo but rather boasted ciphers from a wide range of locales that demonstrated the breadth and depth of their golf scholarships. They seemed to be worn with great pride and coveted like exotic stamps in a passport, with images from obscure but highly regarded clubs as valued as those whose worth was much better known. I also saw that no one wore the logo of the place at which we were playing, even though it is one of the best in the game. And that led me to conclude there is an unwritten rule guiding that practice: Never don the colors of the course where you are teeing it up. Part of that, I am sure, is to avoid feeling some sort of rube who buys his "Paris" T-shirt by the Eiffel Tower, then wears it all over the City of Light. It might stem as well from an understandable desire not to appear too much like a poseur and offend some of the real members in the process.

In time, the conversation turned to what sort of logoed merchandise you should buy when you visit a club. I have always found apparel to be a fine choice, and ditto small items such as ball markers. But it seems pretentious to buy something as significant as a golf bag if it's not your club. Same with items as distinctive as those marvelous knitted head covers at Seminole—such a historic feature of the club that they should be left for those who truly are a part of the clan.

Not surprisingly, the discussion eventually evolved into debates on what makes the best logos. The general consensus at my table was no one liked big logos, especially those so often found overseas that feature emblems the size of bar coasters. We also determined that logos employing characters such as the squirrel at The Country Club in Brookline, Massachusetts, were infinitely better than those made up simply of letters. Now, I do not have as much of a problem with initials as some of my golfing buddies, and I supposed that comes from my West Texas heritage and the fact I always liked the different brands my cowboy kin used to create out of letters to mark and identify their cattle. That's probably why I think the "MC" of the Merit Club in Chicago, for example, is a good look, as are the initials used for San Francisco Golf Club and Caves Valley.

But for the most part, I do favor an icon. And there are so many good ones to admire, starting with the broom-riding witch at Salem Country Club in Massachusetts and the wonderful palm tree from Jupiter Island in Florida. Nothing beats the Mercury boots at Winged Foot, the winged ball at Baltusrol or the retro flag and lettering at Los Angeles Country Club. The milk bottle at MacArthur in Florida is not only visually appealing but also speaks to the history of the land on which Nick Price helped build that course, which rests on an old dairy farm. Then, there's the headless horseman at Sleepy Hollow in New York's Westchester County, near the place Washington Irving made famous with his legendary tome. And what's not to like about the lighthouses at Sankaty Head in Nantucket and Harbour Town on Hilton Head as well as the cow with the golf club in his mouth from Stonewall outside Philadelphia?

As much as I enjoy those images and the clubs they represent, however, I find myself opting more and more these days for shirts and outerwear completely devoid of crocs or calumets. For some reason, no logo has become the most interesting logo to me, and I try to let my actual experiences on the different courses I play—not the symbols sewn into hats and gloves I can buy there—be the best reminders of those wonderful spots.

DISTAFF DISCORD

THE OPPOSITE sex baffles my friend Jenkins on occasion, and it has a lot to do with changes that affect him—and his home life—each holiday season.

"My wife spends 11 months of the year asking me to take things out of the house, like garbage, old newspapers and empty bottles," he explains with an almost dazed expression on his face. "And then in December, she starts asking me to bring things in, like Christmas trees, shopping bags and logs. It goes that way for a while, and as soon as the New Year comes in, we're back to the old routine."

Not surprisingly, this is not the only confusion in Jenkins's life these days. Another source involves the use of bathrooms at the halfway house at his club. Men golfers, it seems, have a tendency to avail themselves of the facilities designated for women there, in large part because they are somewhat closer to the food-and-drink counter than the ones reserved for them around back. (It might also be because of the soothing patterns on the window curtains and knowledge that the ladies' room actually is cleaned on a fairly regular basis.) That has created such controversy and consternation that the club president has charged a two-man subcommittee with finding out why the men insist on using the women's room and what can be done about it. This, of course, is occurring in spite of the fact that the transgressors in this matter always knock before entering the sanctum in dispute and, having been trained properly by their wives, mothers and sisters, fully grasp the importance of putting the seat back down.

Still another source of bewilderment for Jenkins is what once was the men's grillroom in the main clubhouse. A stylish retreat just off the men's locker room, it boasts sumptuous oak paneling, several historic pictures of the club and course hanging on the walls and sweeping views of the links through a pair of bay windows. It had once been an all-male niche where players gathered after their games. Small and unobtrusive with six tables, a TV and fireplace, it was staffed by an attentive bartender and populated by men who interacted with the comfortable air of old school chums. No one spoke, or laughed, too loudly, and the stories were just racy enough. The golfers fancied strong drinks or imported ales, and they rolled dice to determine who bought each round. They had one or two pops at most, and then they were gone.

But all that changed a few years ago when club leaders bowed to the increasingly shrill pressure from distaff members to lift all gender restrictions (except, of course, those preserving Ladies Day). That meant opening up the hallowed men's grill to all comers, and it stands to this day as a reminder of the virtues of progressive and right-minded society.

Not surprisingly, more than a few club members were disheartened by the move. For one thing, the sudden presence of women in their alcove put a serious damper on their often-bawdy jokes and tales. It also forced them to hear lunchtime dissertations on everything from the new Chanel collection to the latest plot lines in *Desperate Housewives*. Then, there was the inevitable influx of toddlers, who added a real Animal House element to the scene by engaging in spirited food fights after loading up on Cokes.

"The men's grill just died after that," says Jenkins. "We only go in there now if it is deserted. Most of the time we gather instead in an adjoining dining area that is almost as charmless as a cafeteria. But at least we have some privacy."

"The couples and kids got the grillroom," he adds wistfully as he contemplates that Diaspora of duffers. "And we got the room they gave up."

It's too bad those fellows feel they cannot lounge in their old haunt anymore. But what's even worse is the inability of clubs to rise to the defense of such important enclaves. After all, men and women have been staking out separate areas for same-sex socializing for centuries, and rooms like the one Jenkins likes to go to after a round have long been enviable and integral pieces of a golf club's fabric. Frankly, it defies all logic and sensibility that they should become too politically incorrect to tolerate anymore.

Just as disturbing is how rapidly an atmosphere has evolved where members are almost afraid to utter the words "men's grill" for fear of incurring the wrath of the equity Nazis. At most places, that phrase appears to have been banished from use forever, a true vulgarity for modern times.

Try as I may, I still do not understand the uproars, for there is little about the concept of a men's grill that should agitate so much. They make up only a tiny percentage of the total square footage of your average clubhouse, do nothing to disturb the overall conviviality of the association, contribute nicely to the bottom line and provide a special service to a demographic group of members in the same way a senior dining discount or junior tennis team might. Men are simply looking for a place where they can drink, lie, opine, and just laugh without having to look over their shoulder every few minutes to see if they are offending anyone. And that sort of refuge has become especially important in a time when it is harder and harder for males to congregate amongst themselves without sounding lurid alarms of chauvinism and exclusivity.

I often hear women lash out at the existence of a men's grillroom, and my best response comes in the form of a question: Why not set aside a similar retreat for ladies and give us all a chance to hang with our homies if we so desire?

"But we don't want a place like that for ourselves," a refreshingly candid female friend intimated not too long ago. "It's just that we don't like the idea of your having one either."

And if you think I am exaggerating that sort of attitude, consider this story from another pal. He founded a very stylish golf club some years ago and then proceeded to do one of the most progressive things imaginable, which was construct not only a men's grill but also a similar spot for female members.

"Well, they weren't exactly similar," he says. "We actually put in a bigger television in the men's grill because we felt more people would be watching in there. Which was indeed the case. But then I started hearing complaints from some of ladies that their TV wasn't the same size."

Jenkins sometimes reflects on how things fell apart at his club. "Twice this past fall, I was eating lunch in our grillroom with a couple of foursomes of men after a round, and we were joking a little bit and telling some good stories. And each time a pair of women walked in and sat at an adjoining table. Now, there were plenty of open seats in other parts of the clubhouse. In fact, we were the only ones eating and drinking in the building either time. But they had to sit right next to us, just to make a point I suppose."

His being a reasonably congenial family club populated mostly by sensible people, nothing violent or confrontational transpired as a result of those encounters. But there were sudden senses of discomfort that felt about as welcoming as a mother-in-law at a bachelor party. The storytelling ground to a halt, the giggling ceased and the room vacated so rapidly you would have thought someone had yelled "Fire!"

"It's not that any of us have any problems with the ladies who came in," Jenkins says. "It's just that they broke up a perfectly good lunch and seemed not to care one bit. Now, if any of us had walked into the same room and came upon a table of women golfers chatting, we would have turned tail immediately and given them their own time and space."

No doubt such a move would have stemmed in part from simple manners and appropriate deference to the people already there. But it also has to do with the fact that Jenkins and his pals would prefer almost anything to crashing an impromptu women's luncheon. Hell, a paraffin pedicure would be more exciting in their minds.

"I just don't understand what enjoyment they would derive from doing something like that," he says.

"Unless, of course, the women have bets among themselves as to how fast the men would leap from their seats when they walked in."

Jenkins frequently wonders how it is that women are not the ones leaping frantically from their seats in his grillroom, and that's because it abuts the men's locker room. And every now and again, a nice midday lunch is interrupted by a door swinging open to reveal several of our more immodest male members wandering around in their birthday suits in what must have looked like something Reuben painted after way too many chiantis (and maybe a hallucinogen or two).

For a time, there was talk of putting a sort of screen on the other side of the locker room door in hopes of terminating those inadvertent flashes, but that was eventually abandoned. And so, eventually, was the grillroom, at least by many of the women who had fought to get it gender neutral. No amount of barrier breaking could make those mealtime displays any more appetizing.

As a modest form of social protest, and as a way to clear his muddled mind, Jenkins stopped dining at his club for a while this past year. But his absence did not prevent him from fretting about the halfway house restroom dispute raging between the sexes as well as the controversy over the grillroom. He had thought of inserting himself in that scrum, perhaps by changing the signs on the rest-room doors as a prank, or suggesting that stand-up urinals be installed in both, making the bathrooms unisex, uniform and, oh so equal. But I had another thought, and that was making a trade, much as the Soviet Unions and United States did in 1962 with their missiles in Cuba and Turkey respectively.

The men would give up the women's bathroom if the women would give up the grillroom. At least during times when either one is populated by members of the opposite sex.

But I have yet to find any takers.

In discussing those hot button issues, Jenkins and I took to pondering deeper matters, and one of the questions we asked ourselves was: Why does equality on the golf course, and in the clubhouse, always seem so selective?

I asked that after a club I know reinstituted a caddie program by mandating the use of loopers on Fridays, Saturdays, and Sundays. The new system was about to take effect when a sage—and obviously liberated— member of the golf committee suggested that caddies also be required on Wednesday mornings, which is Ladies Day, the theory being that what's good for the gander is also good for the goose. Besides, he reasoned, it would also help to get the burgeoning program even higher off the ground and spread support more completely around the club.

Boy, was he wrong!

In fact, his proposal was met with such stiff resistance from the women's golf committee that it was too years before a particularly strong club president was able to get it through the Board of Governors and make it law. The reasons for the adverse reaction ranged from "I don't like caddies watching me play" to "Why should I have to pay for a caddie when I also have to pay for a baby-sitter?" But none of those protesters seemed to have a good answer to" "Why shouldn't female members be compelled to do the same thing as their male counterparts, especially when some of those are single fathers who often have to pay for baby-sitters themselves?"

Actually the whole issue of Ladies Day is an interesting one. I know several clubs that long ago lifted restrictions on when women could tee it up on weekends but still designate a weekday morning when the course can be inhabited only by players of—ahem—a certain gender. And God help the poor soul who forgets what day it is and shows his face anywhere near the 1st tee. I made that mistake once and was rewarded with more dirty looks than a liquor salesman at an A.A. meeting. Needless to say, I beat a hasty retreat to my car, backpedaling like a cornerback moving into coverage, so unsure was I of my safety.

You rarely see backpedaling, however, from one of my favorite clubs, Augusta National, and that is just one of many reasons why I like that retreat—and the people who run it—so much. They have their firm beliefs, they know what it takes to run an efficient and highly rated operation, and they do not get wobbly in the face of ill-conceived criticisms.

Never has that been so apparent than the time a few years ago when the East Georgia club came under serious attack for its membership policies. You see, Augusta National is a men's only association, and that feature has a way of irking certain segments of modern society. The most recent person to take very public offense was a politically active Texan named Martha Burk. As head of an advocacy group called the National Council of Women's Organizations, she wrote the club—and its chairman Hootie Johnson—a letter asking that they change their membership policy, and the club responded with a fierce—and some would say misguided—missive that not so politely told Martha to mind her own business. What ensued was a social and political firestorm that basically engulfed the 2003 Masters and put the very private club much more in the public eye than it ever wanted to be. It was an uncomfortable scene for Hootie Johnson and his cadres and stirred the sort of pathetic pack mentality among media outlets covering the scene that makes it easy for so much of the public to hate the press. One columnist after another jumped in the Martha bandwagon, and it was hard not to read a golf story for a period of time when some writer wasn't ranting from his, or her, soap box, telling the folks at Augusta National how to run their club and what sort of membership policy they should institute. Many of them accused the affable Johnson, as decent and accomplished a gentleman as there is on this planet, of being a misogynistic Neanderthal who would do anything to keep women down on the farm. And Augusta in their views was a bastion of horse-and-buggy prejudice, an old-line Southern club run by a bunch of grumpy old men that had only recently stopped wearing animal skins.

I didn't see it that way in the heat of the controversy. And I still don't to this day. For starters, no one in this land benefits when an organization is attacked and vilified for doing something completely within its legal and Constitutional rights. There are no laws forbidding the creation and operation of all-male clubs and associations any more than there are ones banning those that exist solely for women. In fact, the Bill of Rights protects the ability of all people to assemble peacefully in such ways, so it is both wrong and arrogant for moralistic bullies to gang up on Augusta.

And speaking of morality, spare me the tear-jerking concerns of how Augusta National discriminates. Women are more than welcome at the club, and anyone who has visited when the Masters is not being played can attest to the significant number of women who are there on a regular basis. These females are treated with the utmost deference and respect—on the golf course, in the dining room, and on the range.

That, to me, is not an indication of discrimination (as opposed to male-only clubs that do not permit people of the opposite sex even to walk on the grounds).

So, women are not admitted as members at Augusta. But neither are semiliterate, overly opinionated journalists, and you don't see me clamoring for a spot on that hallowed roster or protesting some perceived prejudice.

Clubs, as a rule, are confined to certain social and economic groups, and what smells like discrimination to the uninitiated is really just a matter of perfectly acceptable exclusivity. Augusta National is for wealthy powerful men who enjoy golf, while the Junior League is for socially conscious, charity-minded women. Look around long enough if you are interested, and you will find a club that is right for you. And if you don't like private clubs or associations, as is the case with many people in this country, then don't join. But please, don't tell me whether it is right for me to belong to one myself.

One of the many arguments made against Augusta National regards its holding of the annual Masters Tournament and the idea that by playing host to such a public event, it should adhere to a different set of standards. But that dog does not hunt. To begin with, the fact that the tournament is a public event has relevance only if the Masters discriminated, which it doesn't. And as a friend recently pointed out, insisting that Augusta diversify its membership because it holds a public tournament is as absurd as demanding that the Girl Scouts of America admit boys because they sell cookies door to door.

Perhaps the thing that upsets me most in how accepting some segments of the public seem to be of political blackmail, which is what is happening in this case. The "Burka Brigade" led by Ms. Burk and her colleagues at the NCWO want Augusta to admit women, and my concern is: what's next? Will they come after clubs that do no have a broad-enough economic base represented in their memberships? Will they demand certain ethnic and religious quotas?

And what good is any of this really going to do? Burk once told me she would drop her campaign if the club let in one female member. She and others argue that it will be an important symbolic move, but in reality, it is nothing more than tokenism of the absolute worse kind.

Equally disturbing has been the role of the mainstream media, which has shown once again how out of touch it is with the rest of the country. For the first four or five months that this issue became all the talk of the sports world, I heard only a handful of people truly support the NCWO's position, while the vast majority seem to side with Augusta National. And a readers' poll taken by *Sports Illustrated* in the midst of the conflict found 89 percent backing the club's position. Yet a good portion of the press, led, of course, by *The New York Times*, devoted inordinate amounts of space to the subject, and to the predictably politically correct positions they took.

Several media outlets, as well as Burk, also found it fun to characterize Augusta chairman Hootie Johnson as a redneck bigot and parody his drawl, as if that has any relevance to the arguments (and would be at all acceptable if it was directed at a demographic group that garners more sympathy than one made up of white, 70-year-old Southern males). That' really progressive, and so is the *Times*' muzzling two of its columnists when they tried to express positions that ran slightly contrary to those on its editorial pages. The *Times* even went so far as to ask Tiger Woods to boycott the tournament as a form of social protest.

As for censoring writers, I only wish the *Times* would follow the lead of my primary employer, *Golfweek*, which allowed me to voice differing views on the subject without worrying that such public dissension would somehow crumble the empire. And instead of asking Woods to take a stand, why didn't the Gray Lady reject all advertising from companies that either entertain at the Masters or have executives who are Augusta members?

Several times during that battle, editorial pundits called on outsiders to solve this case. Some wanted PGA Tour commissioner Tim Finchem to step in, and others called on that ubiquitous loudmouth, the Reverend Jesse Jackson, to get involved. But the only organization that has any business taking care of this subject is Augusta National. And if we don't like what its members do, we can either watch the tournament each April or simply turn off the TV.

That is our right in a free society, as it is Augusta's to run its golf club within the laws of our land. Those exercises are far less damaging to golf—and to the country—than the ones the politically correct police would have us follow.

Personally, I do not care whether a club is "men only," and my preference is always for a place set up for "golfers only," where members truly understand the basic tenets of the game and the pace of play is brisk, the sense of camaraderie strong, and the tone sympathetic and caring. Forget about swimming pools, tennis courts, and fancy restaurants. To hell with Ladies Day, Men's Day, and any other type of special day the uninitiated might want. There is but one grillroom and it's a place where no one blanches at a slightly off-color story. And the first person to suggest holding a summer dance gets asked to leave.

Now, what could possibly confound Jenkins about that?

THE SOUNDS
OF GOLF

MY PLAYING partner had not teed it up for a couple of months, and it showed. Two days into my club's member-guest, we were at the bottom of our flight and grinding only for pride the final two matches. Par for my pal was about as elusive as membership at Augusta National, and hitting a fairway in regulation became cause for major celebration.

In fact, it got so bad that I determined I could no longer watch him hit a shot. So, I began closing my eyes each time he got ready to swing, listening for his club face to strike the ball before lifting my lids to see what sort of disaster he had once again wrought. And it was only then that I truly began to appreciate the many sounds of golf.

The first thing I picked up is how easy it is to discern the quality of a shot simply by the tone, say, of titanium against urethane, or forged steel against Surlyn. A crisply struck ball will produce sensations as melodic as notes from Stan Getz's saxophone. But a Titleist that is toed, heeled, or—heaven forbid—shanked can be as auditorily jarring as a porcelain vase crashing to a concrete floor.

If that initial sound does not tell you everything you need to know about where the ball is going once it leaves the clubface, the verbal revelations that come almost immediately afterward most certainly will. Those are the ones, for example, that exhort the Top-Flite to make miraculous in-flight adjustments. Even the subtlest grunt or groan provides clues to the outcome, and so do the curses that make even the most proper Thurston Howell-look-a-like sound as salty as a sailor. Ditto the frantic cries of "Fore!" that are golf's version of "Incoming!" and prompt normally sensible individuals to contort themselves into ridiculous positions of protection, as if fire ants are scampering across their bodies.

Needless to say, I heard quite a bit of salt from my friend that last day of the tournament, and that got me thinking about all the different sounds of golf I have gotten to know over the years. The good ones abound, and perhaps my favorite is the plop of a ball dropping smartly into a cup, especially if it is for birdie. I also love the "whoosh!" of a swing in a stiff Scottish wind, the golfer suddenly sounding like Zorro with a saber as he brings his driver back and then whips through the ball. The gentle roils of an ocean can be as pleasing to the ears as the Brandenburg Concertos, and a few moments on the 14th and 17th tees at Seminole, for example, are quick

testaments to that. Ditto the noise of the sea lions lounging on the rocks at Pebble Beach or Cypress Points, their
barks melding beautifully with the waves crashing against
the shore. Running rivers and brooks can soothe as well,
as do natural waterfalls at retreats such as Cinnamon Hill
outside Montego Bay in Jamaica, where a round of golf
often feels like a trek through the jungle and a chance
to find a lost civilization, if not a lost golf ball.

But forget about those fake cascades built on a
number of new courses, or those fountains so often
found these days in water hazards. Disney is for family
vacations, not rounds of golf.

My club used to have ringed-neck pheasants prowl-
ing the field grass on the sides of a number of holes,
before the red-tail hawks wiped them out, and it was
always nice to hear the cock birds squawking from their
refuges. Planes are not the sorts of things I normally
enjoy around a golf course. But I have found that many
of my favorite tracks are located near airports, so I have
come to associate good golf with that type of traffic,
whether I am playing Royal Dublin outside the Irish
capital, New South Wales near Sydney, Australia, or
Blind Brook in Purchase, New York.

Some of the best sounds of golf are also the funniest, and near the top of that list is the clopping of a ball
down an asphalt cart path, a bad shot usually becoming
even worse as the person who hit it looks on helplessly.
The loud burble of a three-piecer dropping into the

midst of a water hazard can be as hysterical as a Robin Williams routine, as can the crack of a Pinnacle smacking into a tree. Both of those noises can also lead to the equally diverting spectacle of three golfers trying to suppress—and then ultimately control—their giggling as the fourth in their group battles near fatal apoplexy at the sight of his ball either disappearing into the deep or careening farther off an oak than it had off his clubface.

Certainly golf has its share of bad sounds, and none is quite so horrid as the one of your playing partner blurting, "Your hole," before he has even finished his swing.

I heard that phrase a lot during that member-guest.

Actually, I hear a lot of phrases, both good and bad, during my rounds of golf, and I long ago determined that one of the things I enjoy most about the game is that chatter that goes on among players. I like the jokes and commentaries, the tales and tell-alls, and the biting ways we can get in and out of each other's heads, deflating egos and ruining perfectly good rounds all in one motion.

Most of the folks I tee it up with are pretty good with the quip, and I admire their talents in that regard. But we all have our bad moments, too, and every now and again they come up with some cliché-riddled stinkers. It can be a real yin-and-yang situation, and it has prompted me to think of the best and worst lines I have ever heard on a golf course. Like the one last spring when I played Doonbeg Golf Club in western

Ireland. I had just turned over a punched four-iron into a 30-knot wind so horrendously that it boomeranged into a grassy dune at least two counties away.

"Any chance of finding that?" I asked my caddie with a sheepish grin.

"You could wrap that ball with bacon," he replied in a lovely Gaelic lilt, "and Lassie couldn't track it down."

Clearly, it was time to reload, though I had to wait for the tears of laughter to subside before I actually could see what I was trying to hit.

Moments later, however, after I had put my next ball 15 feet from the pin, I felt like crying again. But this time, it was because one of my playing partners had blurted out that most annoying bromide: "Same guy." Same guy, I thundered to myself as I walked to the green. The second guy was a lot more perturbed than the one who hit first.

My friend Jenkins is a scratch player when it comes to on-course one-liners, and he can send an entire foursome into convulsive giggles with just a few choice words. Such as the time he stepped to the tee of a short par-3 with a 120-yard water carry, looked down at his ball and said: "Hold your breath." Not surprisingly, Jenkins's shot made it across the abyss, but mine ended up in the drink, probably because I was still snickering to myself when I tried to swing.

Jenkins also tells me of the time he was playing the Old Course in St. Andrews when he hit a scalded dog that ran for 150 yards before bouncing off a bunker rake handle, popping into the air after hitting a mound by the side of the green and then clanking off the pin before settling 2 feet from the hole. "Clever" was all his caddie could say after surveying the situation, and that quickly became his watch word for anything that incredibly—and inadvertently—went from bad to good.

Later on, that same caddie stood silently by as Jenkins hit another successful, billiards-like carom and listened to him say: "Golf's a funny game." Responded the looper: "It's not supposed to be."

The wit is not nearly so apparent as the player who hollers, "One time!" as a putt of his snakes toward the hole, especially when it comes after he has already drained three Hail Marys and shot a good five strokes better than his handicap. I also cannot handle the guy who yells, "Bite!" when yet another of his thinned approach shots lands as hot on the green as a F-16 on a carrier deck. And it is particularly bothersome when the fellow urging his ball to "grow teeth" has a handicap in the mid-20s and has never put backspin on a golf ball in his life.

Fortunately, I don't utter too many of those types of threadbare platitudes around my place. Rather, the idea is to come up with something witty and creative, like Steve Ballesteros with a sand wedge. A favorite saying in my regular group, for example, comes out whenever someone hits a putt that either stops 5 feet before the hole or veers wildly off line.

"How did that stay out?"

And if it is said to the right person at the right occasion, it can ensure that the following putt will stay out as well.

One fellow I know quite well is apt to say he's "BIPSIC" when he hits a terrifically bad ball, which translates into "Ball in Pocket, Sit in Cart." A "mother-in-law" is a shot that looks good leaving, and one that fails utterly is a "son-in-law," because it is not what one had hoped for. A ball that is short, ugly, and to the left is called an "Abbie Hoffman," and one with similar characteristics that goes careening to the right is known as a "Rush Limbaugh," (even though he is not particularly short or ugly). And if my friend or anyone else nails a shot off the hosel, he hollers, "Ravi!" as in sitarist Ravi Shankar. I once heard a guy say to that same man, "I have never played this badly before, to which he replied, "I didn't know you had ever played before." And he delights in telling the story of an Irish caddie he once asked: "Will I get there with a 4-iron?" and heard only the one-word reply: "Eventually."

I am generally in the company of friends when I go around my club, but I sometimes find myself spending time there by myself as well, either dining alone on the terrace overlooking our course or racing through a quick 18 in between stories and books. It can be quite entertaining, largely because solitude induces more attentive listening and observing. And, as Art Linkletter might allow, golfers say and do the darndest things.

One of the best places to pick up such pearls is the 19th hole, especially when the rum floats are lubricating tongues like alcoholic versions of WD-40. There was the lady last month, who once sent back a Bombay martini because it was "too strong," and the man who ordered the tuna melt "but without the cheese." Another person I know told a waiter she wanted some pie a la mode, then asked if she could get a little ice cream on the side. And then I heard a forty-something fellow clad mostly in Gucci and Hermes talking about what a tough year he had had in the sort of accent one usually hears at Long island polo games. "I got fired, I crashed my Mercedes and then my girlfriend left me," he lamented with a heavy sigh. "But things are looking up. I have a new job, and Mummy died."

It is much tougher to eavesdrop on the golf course, but a good wind can amplify even the most intimate comments. And an innocent stroll can also produce some real gems. Such as the time I walked by the first tee at my place and heard one of my semiregular playing partners say to his opponent just before they teed up their drives on the opening hole that has out-of-bounds hard to the right: "What ball are you going to be playing for your provisional?"

Then there is the member who recently started a second family with a much-younger second wife. Striding down one of our par-4s, he spied her and their 5-year-old son hitting tennis balls against the backboard by the courts. "I'll be right back," he said with a smile. "I'm just going over to say hello to my son and daughter."

Needless to say, it didn't take long for us to remind him that he didn't actually have a daughter. And yes, he did proceed to reel off a string of very ugly bogeys as we continued to snicker about his faux pas.

Of course, the funniest people are often those who have no intention of being that way. It's just that they cannot help themselves. Like the man who walked up to our greens chairman during a round and complained that our fairways were too bumpy.

However, the winner might be the retiree who was playing with his son against his wife and daughter-in-law one lovely weekend afternoon. The match was tied going into 18, and when the daughter-in-law's drive developed a bit of a tail on the final hole and suddenly drifted toward the fescue, he started screaming, "Go in the rough! Go in the rough! Go in the rough!" And when it disappeared in to the grass, he pumped his fist in the air and hollered a la Marv Albert: "Yes!"

Can you imagine what family dinners are like in that household?

As anyone who has sat on a club board or golf committee can attest, meetings of those groups also can produce some very good material. Jenkins, for example, recounts the time that a very well heeled member of his place once proposed that family members get discounted greens fees when they played. A person could forget for a moment that it costs a mere $80 to bring an unrelated guest to that highly rated track, or that the woman making the inquiry lives in a house the size of an airplane hanger and has a car collection that rivals the Sultan of Brunei's. But who could ignore the absurdity after she added: "It's something that's done at the other five clubs my husband and I belong to."

A few weeks later, Jenkins tells me, during a discussion about what the golf committee should put on the glassware the club often gives out as tournament prizes, that same woman submitted that we only emblazon the Waterford with the club logo and not the date or tournament name. "That way, if you win a lot of crystal during the year, you can always give it away as Christmas presents," she said.

I told that tale to a friend who belongs to a fairly serious golf club, and he said it reminded him of the time his committee was petitioned by a member who rarely, if ever, played. Her concern: the club was spending upwards of $100,000 on a bunker renovation program. "And I don't understand how we can spend that kind of money on this course when there is never enough shrimp to go around during the cocktail hour," she said.

How can you argue with logic like that?

FOREIGN AFFAIRS

ONE OF THE most wonderful things about golf is that it is played throughout the world and can be a fabulous impetus to take to the road and sample the game in faraway places. It can be a spiritual journey, perhaps, to the historic links of St. Andrews and what is widely regarded as the sport's home, or an adventuresome jaunt to Australia, where the great Alistair Mackenzie produced some of his finest designs. Whatever the locale, there is little doubt that golf and travel go together quite well, and a trip overseas with clubs in tow is a very good idea.

The first foreign land I ever teed up in was Ireland, and I fell hard for those links-style layouts that wound along rugged shorelines and among gnarly sand dunes rising several stories high. But I was just as enthused by the clubs themselves, and it did not take long to compile a list of the things that make them great. Even greater, sometimes, than the very best retreats in the States.

Let's start with pace of play, which is so refreshingly quick you might want to do some sprint training before making your trip. No one dawdles on that side of the pond, and I remembered being pushed as a two-some on more than one occasion by threesomes who finished their rounds in about three hours. I sometimes felt I was in a biathlon because I had to stop and catch my breath before each shot.

Starters clad in jackets and ties are a very stylish touch, and so are caddies who say "Cheers," every time you hand a club back to them. I also like the ruddy-faced caddie masters who look as if they have spent a lot of time in the windy outdoors (and the local pubs) and bartenders who can draw a perfect Guinness and then make the design of a shamrock in the creamy head.

The pro shop at Royal Portrush has some of the best logoed merchandise in golf, but what really sold me on that spot was the TV on which *Caddyshack* plays at least twice per day and the staff members who delight in exchanging favorite lines with their cus-tomers. And in the true spirit of Bushwood Country Club, those fellows are happy to throw down a few pints in the evening with thirsty American visitors.

Speaking of Portrush, I love the sod rain shelters built into the dunes throughout the course. They look like crude bomb shelters and give you some inkling of how bad the weather can get. I also had a caddie there who was not only the grandson of the former head profes-sional (and a man who worked at the club for 50 years) but also a member. He knew the course intimately and joined us for a beer when the round was done.

There is a certain whimsy at some places, and what's not to like about clubs that have the word "Royal" in their names and reserve parking spaces for their captains and secretaries. (As a former golf chairman, I would have liked that perk at my home track.) The fabulous course at Pat Ruddy's European Club south of Dublin has 20, not 18, holes. There is also a place on the European Club's scorecard to record what you "should" have shot, and an encouragement for fast play that reads: "Stay Awake. Get Around without Delays. You Are an Athlete!"

But perhaps the most remarkable characteristic of these clubs is their hospitality, especially when it comes to taking care of golfers and the fact that so many good, private institutions willingly open their doors to allow so much outside play. Yes, that allows them to raise revenues and keep club dues and operating costs down, but I wonder how many memberships in the United States would stand for vans of foreigners showing up most every day.

And not to worry if bad traffic—or bad directions—makes you a little late. My mates and I arrived at Royal County Down 15 minutes after our scheduled tee time and were sure we had blown our chance to play one of the world's best tracks. But the starter instantly quelled our fears when he said: "Don't worry, lads, we'll get you off this morning."

What are the chances of that happening at Pebble Beach?

The high quality of Irish clubs also can be measured by what they do not have. For example, I did not see one cell phone that entire first trip. There was nary a tennis court or swimming pool and almost no golf carts or practice facilities. And I never encountered a halfway house. Unless, of course, you count the water fountain on the 10th tee at the Portmarnock Golf Club outside Dublin.

But best of all is that many of those clubs encourage foreign membership for nominal fees. So, now, it is simply a question of deciding which one I should try to join.

Three trips to Scotland in recent years have created even more indecision when it comes to club selection, because that is equally as charming a land and comparably replete with superlative golf courses. I found the country full of character and quirks—as well as some very fine whisky—and overflowing with the very best golf has to offer.

Let's start with the playful noises the seagulls make as they coast above the links of St. Andrews and Dunbar, and the sense they give you of being right on the water. I also liked watching the lobster boats strain across the choppy waters of the North Sea off Crail and

Kingsbarns as I played, and the fields of grain that abut those tracks, reminding us that agriculture is still important in this part of the world and providing much more pleasing sights than those off the condo-lined layouts of Florida and California.

Then, there is the gorse blooming brilliant yellow in the spring and the salty wind howling any time of year. The cathedrals rising from burgs, in which some of the great courses are located, St. Andrews chief among them, enthrall me. It is not only remarkable to gaze at those marvelous structures but also to think of how old some of those buildings are and the fact that these very accessible tracks are not only built right in town but are also critical parts of the social fabric. Farmers and financiers tee it up together, no matter how different their net-worths, and they happily rub elbows in the clubhouse afterward.

It is hard not to love the finishing holes at the West Links at North Berwick and the Old Course in St. Andrews, again playing right into town and having to fret about blocking your drive to the right and watching your tee shot smash the windshield of a brand new BMW. Or the scorecard cover at North Berwick, which features a centuries-old golfing scene that looks like something hanging in the Tate. The so-called pro notes from the course guide at that track serve to amuse as well as inform, and they also put some nasty swing thoughts in your head. On No. 18, for example, the tip reads: "Concentrate, car repairs are expensive. Play it left if you feel the need for safety." After digesting that frightening bit of advice, I nearly put my tee shot on the 274-yard par-4 into the pro shop that stands to the left of the putting green. Well to the left, that is.

I found the massive ball markers I bought at several Scottish courses as charming as the simple white scorecards at the six tracks the Links Trust runs in St. Andrews. Small as a credit card and modest as a monk, they are the ultimate in efficiency and understatement. The wing shooter in me enjoyed the game birds that flushed from the fescue of a number of layouts, the grouse, woodcock, and pheasant startling me on several occasions. And I reveled in some of the outfits my impromptu playing partners wore to the first tee, often threadbare collections of stripes and plaids so horribly matched they would have sent Bill Blass and his best-dressed jury into cardiac arrest.

I enjoyed playing a round with a fellow who told me how his shepard father used to graze his sheep on the Old Course during the winter and chuckled at the subtle ways he proved the Scottish reputation for frugality to be anything but a myth. That morning, I handed him a fresh sleeve of Pro V1s on the first hole, and he said, "I haven't played with new golf balls in years." Then, he promptly put the gift in his bag and teed up a battered ball that looked as old as the game of golf itself.

I came to admire the quick wit of the caddies, especially the one who said, "Scotland is the only country in the world where rainfall is measured in pints," as the heavens opened one afternoon. Another time, after three of us pushed our drives to the same spot on the right of a par-3 at Carnoustie, he asked: "Is there a young lady over there I don't know about?"

Speaking of ladies, I also liked the idea that Scotland has plenty of single-sex golf clubs, some men-only and others reserved strictly for women. It seems highly enlightened in these ridiculous times of political correctness that men can gather sensibly with men, and women with women, without the entire world falling apart. In a similar vein, I thought it made good sense to have spots in the clubhouse designed to accommodate all comers, as Dunbar does, with its ladies lounge, its men's grill, and its mixed grill.

I find that St. Andrews might be the most charming venue in golf, with a slew of great courses in and out of town, wonderful pubs and restaurants, terrific golf shops, and the sort of old-world mystique you would expect from an ancient ecclesiastical center with a university established in 1412.

Yes, that's a full 80 years before Columbus even set sail or the New World.

And not too far away from that spot is my new favorite golf club, in the seaside town of Crail.

Why? First off, there is the name, Crail Golfing Society. The word Crail sounds almost lyrical as it rolls off the Scottish tongue, and "society" makes the association seem even more congenial than your average club. Then, consider its age: founded in 1786, it is the seventh oldest golf club in the world, and just a shade younger than the US of A. Plus, the holes on the Balcomie course offer a great test of golf as well as splendid water views and stone walls built by prisoners of the Napoleonic Wars in the early nineteenth century. In addition, the membership is as welcoming as it is delightful, and guests quickly feel like part of the group.

In fact, it felt that way at every Scottish club and course I played.

Australia was just as convivial a golfing destination but a whole lot harder to get to. Harder in that it took about 20 hours of flying time from my Connecticut home. And I was surprised by many of the things I found there.

Let's start with my arrival in Sydney. I wearily disembarked from the jumbo jet, gathered my bag at the claim area, and began staggering through customs when an officer suddenly pulls me aside.

"Do you have golf shoes?" he asked rather sharply, looking at my travel bag.

"Of course," I replied with something of a puzzled tone, and with that pulled out two pairs of FootJoys. He snatched those from me and hustled through a set of swinging doors.

My first thought, of course, was that he had taken me for a drug smuggler and wanted to see how much contraband I had managed to stash in my shoes. And when the official burst back through the door a few moments later, I could see the problem was indeed grass. Grass, as in the type that grows on the courses I play back home, not the kind that is smoked. Australia, you see, is obsessed about agriculture disease and insists on all golf shoes being thoroughly cleaned and rinsed of any foreign matter before strange strains of bent and poa are tracked across its verdant layouts.

"Here you go," the agent said, handing me two pairs of somewhat soggy shoes that he had scrubbed with soap and hot water. "Have a good day."

I set out to play my first round the following afternoon, at Royal Adelaide Golf Club in the province of South Australia, and it was there I got another interesting taste of the game there. I had just walked out of the pro shop when the general manager came up to me and said, "I am sorry, Sir, but you cannot go out onto the course that way."

Now, I am always careful about proper attire and could not see what was wrong in this case. I wore a collared shirt with the discreet logo of my club back home, Bermuda-length shorts (which I had been told would be fine) and proper—and properly washed—shoes.

What was the problem?

"Your anklets," he said. "You must wear socks that come up higher on your legs."

Back into the pro shop I went, trading in my peds for a pair of veritable tube socks climbing up almost to the middle of my calves and making me look as if I should be hanging around a shuffleboard court. I grumbled slightly about the insistence, but my playing partner explained that it was more or less that way throughout the island continent; you must wear socks that cover the ankles.

And all I could think was: what do the normally freewheeling Aussies have against ankles?

Dress code appears to be a pretty big deal in the big-time clubs a visitor would want to play Down Under, and I have no problem with that. But it was hard not to be amused by a photographic display I came across at the front desk of the New South Wales Golf Club outside Sydney, which looked like the sort of cheesy posters often found in low-rent sushi restaurants to demonstrate what was—and was not—acceptable attire. There were maybe ten examples of players in various states of dress, and some models looked like they had just marched in a Mardi Gras parade. Again, the

Australian fixation with stockings was revealed, as most of the "don'ts" involved socks, whether pushed-down, colored, or striped.

As a rule, Australians have a fine sense of humor, and where else is that better exemplified than in the name of a domestic air service called Emu Air. The emu, you see, does not fly, and that can cause a passenger to take a bit of pause as their jet rumbles down the tarmac for take-off.

It is also evident throughout golf. For example, the people who organized a pro-am I played in before the Jacob's Creek Open in Adelaide seemed only too happy to acknowledge a national passion for most beverages alcoholic by stuffing my goody bag with hangover medicine. They also made light of the high populations of gnats, mosquitoes, and flies that led the countrymen to call the incessant waving of one's hand in front of one's face the "Australian salute" by packing a few tubes of insect repellant in my satchel as well.

And speaking of all God's creatures, it is astounding to see the variety of wildlife in and around the country's finest courses. Several times I came across Koala bears lounging in eucalyptus trees and also saw wallabies and kangaroos as well as two wonderful species of birds called "galahs" and "kookaburras."

Fortunately, I never came upon any of the deadly snakes that are found all over the country. It's actually strange that such a friendly and seemingly benign land can possess so many natural weapons of mass destruction, but it is renowned for its extensive collection of poisonous serpents. And I was warned time and time again to be careful, as I thought of venturing into the rough because a bite from, say, the Australian black snake would likely prove fatal.

It became clear after a while that any golf course superintendents working there would have to be part agronomist and part Marlin Perkins of Mutual of Omaha's Wild Kingdom.

Names throughout Australia are a curiosity, with towns bearing appellations such as Myponga and Yanhahilla. After one round of golf, I ordered a lunch dish called "grilled marron" and asked the playing partner who had recommended it what it was. "Oh, it's just like a yebbie," he said, leaving me even more confused and more than a little concerned about what would be showing up on my plate.

Eventually, I learned a maroon is a type of crayfish, and it was indeed delicious, as was something called flathead fish I had at one spot, and the kangaroo served at another.

The Australian golf clubs I visited, from Royal Melbourne to Bonville International, have wonderful airs about them as well as sensible ways of encouraging reasonable behavior among their members and guests. For example, there's a sign at the 1st tee at New South Wales announcing that visitors must play from the white tees, which provide a course of very modest length and appeal to all but the very best golfers. No five-hour rounds from hackers foolishly determined to tee it from the tips. The powers at venerable Kingston Heath, located in Melbourne's fabled Sand Belt, do not put out benches by the tees for one simple reason: they want to keep players moving (and from sitting). Royal Adelaide has a self-service shoe shine station outside its men's locker room, so if you want your shoes buffed, you have to do them yourself. Perhaps most interesting is the proliferation on golf balls in one-ball packs. That's an Australian tradition, for many games between players are contested over a new golf ball, with the winner getting a signed Callaway or Nike from his opponent with each win.

But best of all for travelers from the United States is that the finest courses in the land, many of which are out on Melbourne's stunning Sand Belt, welcome foreign visitors and encourage guest play.

Now, all you have to do is make it through those long plane trips.

THIS AND THAT

ONE OF THE beauties about life around golf and country clubs is the variety of issues, characters, and situations that regularly present themselves to those traipsing in and out of that world. They may involve the plight of club pros trying to sell shirts and shoes to a persnickety membership or perhaps the inherent difficulty most golfers seem to have in giving a one-word answer to that most basic of questions: What is your handicap? They may even entail simple concerns over dress codes, halfway houses, and the apparently obsessive need for greater length. Of courses, that is.

What follows, then, is a miscellany of ruminations on those and other subjects, different in most ways but nonetheless united by their inherent inanity and amazing ability to raise a brow.

COLLARS, KHAKIS, AND STAYING UP TO CODE

My friend Jenkins and I were having lunch last summer when we were unexpectedly summoned to a meeting with the club president. The problem? A member had gone off the 1st hole clad in a pair of blue jeans. And she had dressed her three children in that same way. The foursome, looking like an advertisement for Levi Strauss, headed out despite the polite protestations of our golf pro and played a quick 9 holes.

Our club has a dress code prohibiting that kind of apparel, so the president asked her to come in for a little chat. Jenkins and I are on the board, and we arrived just as our fearless leader was delivering a stern lecture about abiding by the rules regarding course attire (as this was not her first violation). A half-hour later, I was back at lunch, feeling pretty good about the intervention. After all, we seemed to have made a strong impression on the deviant member and sent a message to the rest of the club by confronting her. We knew word of the incident would seep out and serve as a not-so-subtle reminder for members to pay attention to what they wore on the course.

But Jenkins seemed uncharacteristically distraught as he picked at his lobster salad, and soon explained why.

"I hate the idea of belonging to a club that has to have a dress code," he said. "You would think we'd only let in people who knew what to wear on a golf course."

On the surface, it seems a simple enough issue. Either you learn early in life what to don for a round of golf by caddying, for example, or following the lead of your golfing parents or grandparents. Or you figure it out as you go along, perhaps by observing what other people at the club wear or talking to the pro about the general code of attire. Touring pros are not necessarily a bad place to go for fashion tips so long as you stay away from items such as mock T-shirts, which look fine on a buff Tiger Woods but are as unseemly on an over-weight 16-handicapper as his golf swing. And under no circumstances should you consider those Tabasco golf shirts, which look as if they were made from drapes that hung in a New Orleans bordello.

Sadly, such logic appears to be way too deep for many country clubbers to fathom. You see it in the knuckleheads who show up on the first tee in black bicycle shorts or T-shirts from the latest Metallica concert. You find it in the bums so sloppily attired they look like unmade beds. And you wonder why they seem incapable of adhering to Jenkins's basic adage for golf course dress: Wear what you wore when you were trying to get into the club in the first place.

However, even approved articles of clothing can cause consternation. Like golf hats, which look fine on the course but should never be worn inside. Most members at my club pride themselves on their good manners. Yet, I frequently see some keeping their lids on right through lunch. I'll make some snide and rather audible comments about the practice on occasion, but those never work as well as the time a friend's nearly

4-year-old son looked at two middle-aged captains of industry eating lunch with their caps on and said in a loud voice: "Daddy, what does a gentleman do when he walks into a room?"

"He takes his hat off," his father replied, and much chagrined, that's exactly what those fellows quickly did.

Shorts are another matter altogether. Even though I often wear Bermudas in the summer, I struggle at times with their place on the golf course. Part of that comes from having a father who never wore shorts on the links. His view, shared by many of his generation, was that shorts were for children, and you stopped dressing in them when you were old enough to go to the bathroom by yourself. Real men, the thinking went, wore slacks at their clubs, unless, of course, they were playing tennis or swimming.

For many years, some of the finest clubs in America did not allow shorts on their courses, but only a few enforce that policy today. One such place is Augusta National, and its long-held view on that subject is best demonstrated by a classic Clifford Roberts story. One morning, it seems, the longtime Augusta chairman spied a club member walking outside the clubhouse in a pair of Bermudas. "What are you doing today, Charlie?" Roberts asked. The response was, "Playing golf," and Roberts's simple retort was, "Where?"

I know, some folks might bristle at the necessity of a dress code, and I can understand the aversion to conforming to what can no doubt be viewed as nonsensical norms. But my feeling is, if you don't like dress codes, then don't join a club that has them.

Obviously, some people don't like to be told what to wear no matter where they play, and musician Willie Nelson counts himself among that group. One time, he and a few of his band mates appeared at a daily fee course in Florida clad in blue jeans and T-shirts, only to be told at the first tee that they did not have "proper attire." So Nelson took his friends back to the pro shop, and asked the clerk if everything sold there was indeed "proper."

"Absolutely," the man replied.

Nelson then bought several outfits for his friends in the women's department, and they soon reappeared at the tee, dressed this time in halter-tops and skirts. The pro tried to stop them again, but Nelson would have none of it.

"You said these clothes were all proper attire," he exclaimed.

And off they went, striking a victory for social protest and creating a dress code loophole through which others can walk.

But only if they have the legs.

HALFWAY THERE

As a rule, I am not a big fan of halfway houses. I guess that's because I hold the Old World view that no golfer ever needs to break for gingersnaps and Gatorade if he, or she, is playing at a proper pace. After all, how hard can it be to go without sustenance for three or four hours?

Unfortunately, that's a dissenting view on this side of the pond, where halfway houses proliferate like hecklers in a Colin Montgomerie gallery. To be sure, some places have sensibly resisted the need to build and operate such on-course commissaries and believe a few strategically placed coolers or water fountains do the trick. But most of our golf and country clubs feel compelled to offer more food and beverage options than a Wolfgang Puck restaurant. And whether we like it or not, halfway houses have become as much a part of the American golf experience as cart paths and GPS systems. Which means, of course, that we have to deal with them.

And if we have to deal with them, I suppose we can find a way to find some good in their existence. A bottle of cold water during a hot summer round is a fine idea, especially after a night of Dark and Stormies, and a few Ritz crackers and some peanut butter make up nicely for missed breakfasts. Plus, halfway houses are infinitely better than those hideous beverage carts that patrol many layouts.

As for the things that make some halfway houses better than others, I prefer the ones with the smallest structures and most simplistic menu offerings. Hot food seems an unnecessary luxury, and an unhelpful one at that; some folks crave hotdogs between nines, but I don't know anyone who can pure a long iron after ingesting one.

My friend Jenkins believes the best halfway houses are those that aren't really halfway at all, which is the case at Pine Valley and Sleepy Hollow. The Yankee in him loves the stop at Wayne Huizenga's place called The Floridian because the food and drinks there are free. And while free is not a word you ever hear at the sort of miserly New England club to which he belongs, he believes there is something quaint about a spot that is unmanned and exists entirely on the honor system. Like the one at Chicago Golf.

The halfway house at my home track is an attractively austere building that has a loft caddies once used as an off-course retreat. It was also a lair from which they would mutter mild insults to unsuspecting club members. "Looks like you've gained a little weight, Mr. Barney," they'd say, as Mr. Barney would wait to get his cup filled. And he would look around to see who had said such a thing as his server anxiously cringed and waited for the next overhead comment.

Another favorite trick was for the caddies above to talk while the boy manning the counter moved his lips, creating scenes reminiscent of those Kung Fu movies where the words and mouth movements never seemed to jibe.

Perhaps the best thing about our halfway house is that it is located by the tee for the par-3 11th hole and is therefore a perfect betting venue, the usual play being: farthest from the pin buys. That may not sound like a big deal, but when you factor in drinks and snacks for four players and a pair of caddies, a bad shot can cost $20. And none of that can be applied to the monthly minimum.

Needless to say, some golfers don't handle that pressure very well, and I have friends who haven't hit the 11th green in regulation in years. Others have become so desperate that they try to reverse the bet so that closest to the hole pays. But then they hit their shot stiff and lose just the same.

The betting can get a little intense, as it did the time that two of our more senior members hit their tee shots in the water and proceeded to get into a terrific argument over whose Top-Flite went into the drink closer to the pin. Ten minutes of haggling nearly brought play to a standstill, and two old friends to blows. However, cooler heads prevailed when a following foursome resolved the dispute by picking up the halfway house tab and sending the near combatants on their way.

JUST GIVE ME A NUMBER

There is only one question in the English language that is impossible for golfers to answer with a single word, and that is: What is your handicap?

It doesn't matter if it is being asked at stylish Cypress Point or at some beat-to-hell muni on the Jersey Shore. It doesn't make any difference if the person being queried has the bluest blood in Boston or a lineage that includes consecutive generations of felons. If he plays this wonderful game, he is incapable of providing a simple number and leaving it at that.

"Well, I'm an eight now, but I was a six at the start of the season," a reply might begin. "Then I hurt my wrist taking out the garbage a few weeks ago and really can't turn the ball over. Actually, I should be a ten."

Or you have the self-proclaimed comedian who wants to show everyone what a wag he is. "My handicap?" he asks. "It's my bad breath, and a very short . . . attention span."

Multiply either of those comments by four, and you have the weekend morning scene at most first tees in the country, with some poor slob holding a scorecard and pencil as he desperately tries to discern the pertinent stroke information while listening to more obfuscation than a presidential press conference.

And you'd think any riddles about handicaps would quickly be solved once play actually starts. But people rarely seem to have the handicap they say they do. There are 15s who drill their drives 290 yards down the middle and 5s who dribble tee shots between their legs. I know of clubs dominated by sandbaggers whose handicaps are so criminally high they should be in wit-

ction programs. I once played against a member of one such club and thought we had a pretty good game going until he had a 60-yard pitch to the hole on No. 15. But then he asked his caddie not only to mark my ball, which was only a few feet from the cup, but also to take out the stick. Then the man, who said he was a 14, damn near holed the shot. He went on to win the remaining three holes, leaving me $10 poorer and more than a little chagrined. But he was just one of the guys at his place, because to them, golf was mostly about winning.

Conversely, there are clubs where vanity is king, and the handicap numbers are much lower than they should be. Too bad if someone loses a $20 bet on a Saturday game; they still have that six in the computer, which in their mind is akin to pulling up in a fully loaded Lexus. We have a few of those at my place, and it is always a hoot watching them on the 1st hole. They conduct deep discussion about their respective indexes, all of which are as out of sync with reality as their perceptions of their own games, and then they play from the back tees. Problem is, there is hardly a time when more than one of those hackers actually lands a ball in the fairway, and that's with everyone taking at least one mulligan.

It must be mentioned, of course, that even the most honest golfers can suddenly get hot or cold, and there is nothing the rest of us can do when that happens but cringe. Such as the time a colleague, a legitimate 16 handicapper, played Carnoustie in a foursome that included a Scottish acquaintance and shot 110. Flash forward to Royal Birkdale a year later. The Scotsman had invited the American, still a 16, to join several U.K. journalists in a Stableford event. This time, the 16 carded a 78, won all the money, and nearly got lynched.

"They all wanted to kill me," my friend recalls with a wry smile. "But they were really after the guy who had invited me."

While having too high a handicap can be hazardous to your health, having one that is too low can be just as dicey, as my friend Jenkins learned one day last summer when he came home to announce he had dropped to a one. He beamed proudly as he delivered the news, but his wife quickly put him in his place.

"You ought to be embarrassed to carry a handicap that is lower than the number of children you have," she said. Then she handed him a kid.

PROS DON'T WORK PRO BONO

I don't remember my father ever talking to me about finances, and he was not much on articulating the intricacies of a happy marriage. After all, Dad was a laconic guy, true to the rugged introversion of his generation and not at all prone to deeply meaningful discussions.

But there was one subject he was not shy about exploring, and that deals with a certain issue of behavior whenever he or any of his four children walked into a golf shop.

"Make sure you buy something from the pro."

It didn't matter whether the purchase was as small as a sleeve of golf balls. The idea was to support the man or woman behind the counter, and our father frequently reminded us that as members of a club, we had a responsibility to buy all—and he meant all—our gear from that person. He also made it clear that the edict applied to those places we visited as guests, and Dad often bought me a shirt or sweater I didn't really need at those spots, so adamant was he in pursuing that policy.

The obvious rationale to him was that the pro depended on those purchases to make his living. And being part of a club meant supporting it—and its employees—in every possible way, whether that entailed buying all your woods and irons there or eating lunch in the clubhouse after a round even though you might get a better—and more expedient—repast somewhere else. Buying from the pro also was a way to ingratiate oneself with that person, which often ensured exceptionally good service and maybe even a 1st-hole start for the member-guest shotgun.

I know that pros certainly appreciate that kind of consideration, and they are keenly aware of which members buy from them regularly. As for those folks who feel compelled to shop elsewhere, the animus can run pretty high. I remember watching a new member stroll into a shop at a club I know carrying a plastic bag brimming with products he had just bought at an off-course retailer. And I was not at all surprised when the head pro nearly jumped over the counter at the guy. I don't think he had physical harm in mind, but the pro was clearly anxious to give the fellow the sort of education I received from my father, though probably in much more pointed fashion.

I only started playing golf with any sort of regularity after college, and true to my father's wishes, I made it a point of making a purchase every time I walked into a pro shop. Broke as I was back then, I usually opted for something modest, like a golf glove. But as time went on, I began digging deeper, eventually moving up to a higher-end category of sweaters and such.

After a time, however, I noticed I had a problem. Not only did I possess enough golf shirts and wind breakers to fill a Fairway & Greene warehouse, but also I was starting to feel the financial pinch from making so many $100 purchases. I mean, I was all for taking care of the pro, but not at the expenses of taking care of myself.

So, I started to downsize, first moving to less expensive hats and repair tools and eventually settling on ball markers. For one thing, I liked their $2 price tags and the fact that they carried the logo of the place I was playing. They were also easy to pass along as gifts, and oftentimes

I grabbed a handful and doled them out to my pals—and pros—back at my course. I also enjoyed collecting them, and it is fun reaching into the pocket of my bag before a game and seeing which of the 200-odd markers I pull out for a particular round. There are always some old favorites, to be sure, and a few surprises as well.

What is not surprising is the feeling that I surely take my near-obsessiveness with pro shop buying too far at times. A few years ago, for example, I was not able to find any long golf tees at the shop at my club, which compelled me to make a trip to the local discount outlet. As soon as I pulled into the parking lot, I felt as uncomfortable as if I had just driven up to a brothel. I looked around as I opened the car door, making sure I didn't see anyone I knew, and then scampered into the store. Fortunately, I found the long tees quickly, and after grabbing two packets, I scurried back to my car. Then I hustled down the road, feeling a bit cheap and dirty and wondering what to do with the plastic bag emblazoned with the name of the off-course golf shop I had just patronized.

It may have been only golf tees. But my father, you can be sure, would not have been pleased.

FIT TO BE TIED

Golf customization is in, and that means club fitting is all the rage. I have gone through the process with a few major equipment makers, mostly in the line of duty as a golf writer, and watched dozens of other recreational players do the same. Obviously, there are tangible benefits to having a set of woods and irons made to your exact specifications. But they do not always outweigh the silliness of the process.

Let's start with perhaps the greatest problem with a proper club fitting, which is the use of video to observe and understand a golfer's technique. The question is simple: Does anyone other than a top amateur or touring professional really want to know what his swing looks like?

The answer for me is an emphatic No!, largely because I long ago decided there were two things I never wanted to see myself doing on video, and one of them was trying to hit a golf ball. My primary fear is that a screening of such a mortifying exhibition easily could shatter whatever tenuous confidence I have in my game. It could also send me into a handicap death spiral that would not end until my current USGA index of three falls into the mid-20s.

Lest you think I am overreacting to the potential sight of my rather hideous hack on the big screen, consider a friend of mine who also happens to be a PGA club professional. He tells me he long ago eschewed the use of video in his teachings for fear his members would be so discouraged by what they saw that they would give up the game.

Tennis anyone?

Another concern with the golf swing on tape is whether any of us weekend amateurs are good enough— or possess the necessary time and dedication—to do anything about the flaws we discover. I assiduously avoid the range in favor of 18 holes with friends, and the course is no place to work out the problems your club fitter has pointed out on tape. So, I simply stick with what I know, no matter how ugly it might be.

As anyone who has been through a club fitting knows, the process invariably involves a great deal of ball hitting. That, of course, is a good thing, but I often wonder how accurate a reading of our swings the equipment makers actually get. For example, on a recent trip to a company's test center, I warmed up for an iron-fitting session with a launch monitor by striping a dozen or so 3-irons, each crisply hit and curving slightly right to left with a delectable baby draw. But then I stepped to the stall with the launch monitor, and suddenly turned into David Duval, with balls going every which way but loose. The more I tried to concentrate, the worse I seemed to get. That prompted my fitter to remark that the 5-yard stretch between the place where I was hitting my warm-up shots to the area measured by the launch monitor was "the longest walk in golf." And he tried to assuage my shattered ego by recounting the story of another golfer who needed nineteen swings to come up with three that were good enough for the actual fitting. "And that was a week after she won the Nabisco," he added.

Of course, the best part of any club fitting is finally receiving the finished product, the shiny new sticks that usually appear with a personalized golf bag or rain suit and sundry accessories that make the day of arrival feel like Christmas.

Initially, the new toys feel very good. But whatever glow I have over clubs that fit like a tattersail from Turnbull & Asser quickly disappears when I realize I have essentially eliminated any outside excuse for poor play. It can no longer be feasible to blame the irons for a bad shot, or a bad round, and the necessity of truly facing the music of an occasionally horrid golf game can be a daunting task for someone so firmly entrenched in denial, and so quick to avoid personal responsibility for a topped 3-wood.

Sometimes, I think it would be better simply to buy off the rack.

TEEING OFF ON LENGTH

The two guys at the club bar are talking excitedly about the warming weather because they know it is nearly time to hit their first drives of the year. It is spring, and these New Englanders appear very fired up indeed.

Fired up, that is, to play their home course, a charming layout built in the early 1900s. But they dread the choruses of nonsense that inevitably accompany their return to the links. The blather emanates from a cadre of club members who incessantly beseech the golf committee to stretch out their track like a piece of Silly Putty. Their testosterone-laden goal, it seems, is to transform a stylish, Jazz Age course into Bethpage Black at U.S. Open time, and use that as a way of flexing their golfing muscles.

"It's all we hear from those people," says one of the fellows at the bar, a septuagenarian who once played to a four handicap and also served for many years as head of his club's greens chairman. "They keep wanting to add length, and for what? To brag to their friends that they have the longest layout around?"

I sympathize with that man's frustration, because we sometimes deal with the same issues at my place. Granted, those are the sentiments of only very small segments of both memberships. But they are very vocal segments, loudly fretting that historic tracks created before the introduction of steel shafts and triplex mowers will become obsolete if they don't undergo a Barry Bonds-type makeover.

They also worry there is something embarrassingly inadequate about a golf course that in their mind doesn't quite measure up in length.

No amount of noise, however, can obscure the fact that such pleas for transformation are not only misguided but also would ruin some of the country's great old courses and destroy the enormous pleasure so many members derive from their homey club layouts.

Consider that only a tiny percentage of any club membership plays the back tees on a regular basis. And even at places with very strong ranks of amateur players, there is at best an infinitesimal number for whom additional yardage might truly and sensibly improve the challenge—or experience—of a particular hole.

To be sure, it is a different situation for those tracks playing host to PGA Tour events or top amateur competitions, for when you bring in those types of players, you had better have some length. But adding yardage there makes sense because it is genuinely needed and is done for the tournament itself.

Why, then, are so many knuckleheads pushing for the big distance changes on basic membership courses?

Ego is a huge part of it, as is an inherent delusion among golfers that they are much better than they actually are. Attitude is also an issue. In my part of the country, for example, we have a lot of big-money business moguls who get the numbers on their 1040s confused with their IQs. So, there is so dissuading them when they get it in their heads that their home tracks need to be Tiger-proofed even though Tiger Woods will never play there.

A course architect recently complimented the restoration work we are doing on my home track, a lovely Seth Raynor layout, for being geared toward the members who play it all the time, and not for the greater game of golf. In other words, he likes that we are not trying to attract a U.S. Open, or even a U.S. Junior. Rather, we are simply revitalizing and enhancing the wonderful attributes and features of a historic gem. The idea is simply to make it an even better place for the members, for people like those two fellows at the bar—longtime golfers who have neither the physical nor psychological need for something that measures 7,400 yards from the tips.

If only we could get all those guys oozing testosterone to think the same way.

SENSIBILITIES LOST

My friend Jenkins recently returned from a ten-day golf tour of the British Isles, and he was depressed. His mood, however, was not an accurate indication of how his trip had actually gone. The courses he had played were first-rate, and the weather uncharacteristically calm. He had also managed to find his "A" game along the way as he developed a newfound appreciation for single malt whisky and a closer connection to the other members of his traveling foursome.

So why was he feeling blue?

"Because I cannot believe how far from the sport we have gotten back here," he said, referring specifically to his club in the Northeast as well as golf throughout the United States. "I was home a week and suddenly wished I could just return golf to where it used to be."

The thing that initially set off Jenkins, who sits on his club's golf committee, was a confrontation he had with a fellow member before the jet lag had even worn off. "This guy started complaining that our greens were not running at some ridiculously high number," he recalls. "And I got to thinking that in all the times I have been to Ireland or Scotland, I've never heard a person complain about slow greens, even though that may have very well been the case. They were what they were, which was fine for us, and an occasional bit of sluggishness did nothing to detract from the overall experience."

So, instead of being able to savor that sojourn for any amount of time, Jenkins had to contend with an ill-informed dolt pining for Augusta-like perfection and putting surfaces that were slicker than toboggan runs.

I understood my friend's dismay, as I have seen and felt the same deterioration of sensibilities, with caution and modesty thrown far too often to the wind. It is a dangerous development that saps the enthusiasm of even the most ardent players and loses touch with what the sport is all about. It also damages the economic health of clubs and courses trying to keep up with the high maintenance whims of a golfing public that seems to want to make the game as ludicrously over-the-top as a Las Vegas hotel.

I see it even in something as innocuous as pull carts. No, not those old-fashioned trolleys you still find at tracks such as Connemara or North Berwick, mind you, but rather the modern models whose high-tech designs and hefty power batteries make them appear as fully loaded as Ferraris and entirely capable of completing the Rabat-Dakar rally with only one recharge.

As a rule, I think "pampering" is fine in a spa, but I do not understand how anyone figures we need that at a golf club. Yet there are no shortages of so-called valets and concierges at clubs and resorts all over this country, hopelessly officious people who scramble from car to car and everywhere in between, grabbing bags and shoes and anything else they think you might need for a round. Personally, I am only too happy to carry my own Burton to the pro shop and really don't need anyone else to assist me other than a locker-room attendant who is nice enough to shine my shoes while I am playing and a bartender who will draw me a tasty ale afterward.

After all, I am only looking to play 18 holes, not to get a Golden Door seaweed wrap.

But simplicity is getting harder and harder to find.

I notice clubs that run enough electricity through their halfway houses to light Shea Stadium at night just so they can offer a sumptuous selection of hot food from a menu as well assembled as the one at Le Cirque. I also rue the trend toward clubhouses the size of Loire Valley chateaus and wish we would celebrate instead those delightfully diffident retreats found at clubs throughout the Old Country.

Sadly, this list only touches on all that has gone wrong, I know of places where members cancel club tournaments if, Heaven forbid, the wind is blowing too hard, or the course is slightly wet. Problem is, it matters not one bit to the organizers if the track is still open to play for everyone else, they'll be damned if they have to play in anything but perfect conditions.

And playing a simple four-ball, it seems, has gone completely out of style, and you need a professor of mathematics to discern from your annual schedule of club events when it is possible to play a basic Nassau match with your friends.

Jenkins shook his head as he and I discussed these many concerns, and then he got a call about just one more.

"Why don't we get a new television in the grill room?" the member said in a tone that made his words sound more like a demand than a request. "I think we need one of those plasma TVs with a big screen."

My friend could not turn back the clock fast enough.

BE A GOOD GUEST (AND BEWARE THE HOST FROM HELL)

Of all people in golf, none are quite so revered in some circles as the fellow who belongs to the very best clubs in the land and is only too happy to share his great fortune—and superlative courses—with his friends.

Call him the golf host.

You know the person, the one who through business success, family connections or sheer luck has managed to ensconce himself on the membership rolls of, say, an Augusta National or Cypress Point. And for the vast majority of golf slobs like myself, they are our only access to such hallowed grounds.

Experience tells me there are two kinds of golf hosts. One is the good friend with whom you would play even if his only membership was the rattiest goat track in town. Not only is he fun to be around and exceedingly generous when it comes to inviting you for a game, but he also has the class to suggest you fill the foursome with a couple of your best mates. Many times, that member is only too happy to pick up the greens fees and even buy lunch, expecting no more in return than some good manners and your taking care of his caddie. To be sure, he anticipates—and no doubt deserves—more if the outing entails an overnight stay as well as dinner, wine, and who knows what else. But that's taken care of by splitting the bill among all participants.

These types of golf hosts clearly love the game, and they delight in showing newcomers around their vaunted clubs. And the more oohs and aahs the better, because the golf host truly appreciates how much guests appreciate being let in the door.

The second kind of golf host can be a bit dicier, however, because he is not generally someone who 1) you know very well or 2) is a person with whom you would normally tee it up. And that can lead to problems, most frequently in the form of a guy who never seems to let you forget he is doing you a big favor and clearly expects you not only to pay all of your expenses but his as well. There also is the distinct possibility that this person is the worst kind of horse's ass on and off the course and the sort of character his admissions committee would gladly blackball if it could do it all over again.

Now, some observers would say that lining up with a buffoon like that is an occupational hazard of the golf mooch and his quest to play the very best, but I hate to think my friends and I are so shamelessly desperate as to sink to that level. But then again, what wouldn't most of us do to get on Merion?

Besides, the real focus of our attention should be on our behavior before, during, and after the much-desired round, and not necessarily that of our host. And there are several ways to go in that regard. For starters, the golf mooch should make sure he dresses properly and knows what to wear throughout the outing. (Long pants during the round, if that's what the rules call for, and a blazer in the clubhouse for lunch or dinner afterward, if that's the usual routine.) Gifts of thanks are a good idea as well, but don't fill the shopping cart in the pro shop a la Rodney Dangerfield in *Caddyshack*. (One box of naked lady tees will certainly do.) Leave the cell phone at home, let the host set the game and bets, and generally praise his shots—and hospitality. But try not to sound too much like Eddie Haskell buttering up Mrs. Cleaver. Tip members of the club staff when appropriate, and overtip if warranted. Make sure you thank the golf professional when you leave and tell him how well his staff treated you.

It is always important to be on time, something a friend of mine once found impossible on a trip we took to Pebble Beach. Our host graciously took us to Cypress Point three days in a row, and my golfing partner was so consistently tardy when it came to leaving in the morning that he soon was dubbed "The Phantom." We ribbed him hard about that for most of the trip, and the kidding was good-natured. But you could tell our golf host was getting annoyed after three days of constant waiting, and the line he uttered when we left— "I filled up your car with gas so I'd make sure you guys got out of here today"—spoke volumes.

Finally, be a good sport, even if you are playing like a dog. Hosts rarely take kindly to club throwing, and part of the focus of the golf guest during the trip should be on getting invited back. Have plenty of cash on hand (the great clubs do not have ATMs in their pro shops), and pay whatever bills you receive for your trip on time. And write a thank-you note. Immediately.

Many of the best golf hosts have a wonderful habit of establishing regular trips to their clubs, and it is not at all unusual to see those types of groups at places like Pine Valley, good friends coming back year after year to relish the camaraderie and the golf in such an enviable setting. It is also a fairly common occurrence to see those groups break up, due to the tragic passing or gradual demise of the fellow who traditionally led the expeditions. Nothing is quite as chilling in the mind of a good golf mooch, and that not only carves a heart-wrenching void in his life but also leaves him very much in the lurch when it comes to that regular outing at Seminole.

The only thing he can really do when that happens is start a semitasteless search for another golf host, and another way in the door.

A MYSTERIOUS YET FASHIONABLE FELLOW

He is a stylish chap, clad in top hat and morning coat and sporting a bow tie. His left hand clutches a pair of gloves, and his right holds a slender cane upon which he leans. He is middle-aged, of English lineage and found at many of the best golf retreats in the world.

He is Clubman.

Only Clubman is not actually a man. Rather, he is a brand, of hair tonics, talcum powders, and after-shave lotions that fill locker rooms everywhere. You know the products, with the pale green background and red lettering and the natty Clubman trademark, lined up with those ancient tubes of Brylcream and alongside those jars of combs soaking in that industrial blue solution.

I've seen Clubman around my place for years and always wondered who owned the company and where the products were made. I was also curious about the places they were sold as I never found a Clubman canister of spray deodorant or shaving cream anywhere other than the actual clubs themselves. It all made me feel a little like the title characters in *Butch Cassidy and the Sundance Kid*, thinking: "Who are those guys?"

So, I began nosing around, first by picking up a bottle of Clubman cologne and looking on the label for an address. It read: "Clubman Pinaud, Los Angeles, Ca.," and I went right to directory assistance. But there was no listing for either name in all L.A. Next step was an Internet search, but all I got there were names and numbers of various Clubman distributors. Still no information on the company headquarters and someone who could tell me all about it. Finally, I went to the general manager of my club, who put me in touch with the man who sells Clubman in our area, who put me in touch with the company itself.

I figure it would be easier to get the specs for the next generation Pro V1.

My source was Bill Kochanski, manager of the Clubman brand, and first he provided me with a little history. He said it all started with a company called Pinaud, which began making a line of men's toiletries in the United Kingdom in the early 1800s. The products used only the finest essences and ingredients and were sold primarily through high-end stores. At some point, Pinaud developed Clubman as an offshoot brand, and that was sold mostly in barbershops and barbershop boutiques. By the 1940s, it had become a staple in those locales, as well as in selected retail outlets. But according to Kochanski, it had yet to make its way into golf and country cubs.

All that began to change in the mid-1970s, when a privately held, Los Angeles-based company called American International Industries and its president, Zvi Ryzman, purchased the Clubman brand.

Rzyman has moved to expand the number of Clubman offerings as well as the places where the brand can be found, including clubs and also major chains such as Wal-Mart and Walgreen's. It also is doing very well internationally, and Clubman products are currently sold throughout Central and South America as well as Europe and the Middle East.

What, then, makes Clubman such a popular fellow? Many of my golf partners say it is the smell of the different products, and Kochanski says he understands the appeal. "The classic Clubman scent has not changed much over the years," he explains. "It has a citrus, woodsy top note, and on the second level it is mostly musk. Plus, many of the fragrances we use today, whether it's Bay Rum or Quinine or Eau de Portugal are pretty much the same ones that were used way back in the early nineteenth century. We have modified them some, but we really haven't changed them. And it has been important to keep the line more or less intact along the way and as original as possible."

For as long as most people can remember, Clubman was geared toward a definitely middle-aged crowd, the 40-and-over set who liked to go to places like country clubs and golf clubs. And A.I.I. wants to keep it that way. But Kochanski says the company is branching out to a younger set, starting with a series of hair grooming products known as Clubman U.S.A. Sport.

It's nice stuff, but Clubman himself is nowhere to be found on the label.

Clubman without the Clubman?

Not to worry, says Kochanski. Clubman will always be around to serve us traditionalists.

GOLF IN PERSPECTIVE

AS ANYONE who knows my work can attest, I get more than a little aggravated with some of the things that go on in the world of club golf. In fact, I become downright enraged when I have to witness yet another example of boorish and unfeeling behavior on the course or in the clubhouse, and it's often enough to send me right to the pharmacist for one of those chemical cocktails designed to lower my blood pressure as it also eases my anxiety. Just being around the game, it seems, can be a stressful proposition.

But I never get peeved at golf itself. Actually, I cannot think of a sport I enjoy as much, and none commands so much respect from the people who play it as well as those who watch professionals and top amateurs compete, whether in person or on TV. And that respect is one of the primary things that makes golf so different from any other recreation I know.

Perhaps nothing sets golf farther apart in that regard than its demand that players police themselves and take

full responsibility for adhering to the rules as promul-
gated by the game's governing bodies, either the United
States Golf Association (in the United States and Mex-
ico) and the Royal & Ancient Golf Club of St. Andrews
(for the rest of the world). And there clearly is not
another game in which abiding by those regulations is
such a critical part of playing—and competing.

Take a sport like baseball. Think of the stories of
pitchers scuffing up balls before pitching them, or out-
fielders knowingly trapping line drives and doing all they
can to fool umpires into thinking they actually made the
catches. Ever see a base runner who knew he was tagged
out on a play but was ruled safe anyway turn to the
umpire and say: "I'm sorry, but I was out. I am going
back to the dugout now"? The answer is no, because
that sort of attitude doesn't exist in baseball. Instead, the
concept is to try to get away with as much as possible.

Sadly, that has become something of an institutional
attitude, especially if you consider baseball's recent problems with steroid abuse. Not only does it appear that
dozens of major league players, including some who will
no doubt be first-ballot Hall of Fame candidates, have
been using a wide variety of banned, performance-
enhancing drugs over the years, but that utter corrup-
tion of the rules has occurred with the acquiescence of
all factions running the game, in other words the
owners and players' union. Once, that sort of sleaze
was associated only with Third World dictatorships,

organized crime operations, and their ilk. But now, it sullies what once was our National Pastime with one cheating scandal after another, making a formerly proud recreation feel as cheap and sordid as a "by-the-hour" motel.

While most other sports have not sunk to that level, they do share that sense that anything goes on the field or court so long as you don't get caught. You do what it takes to win, and what National Football League offensive lineman hasn't held, tripped, or slammed opponents throughout a game in an effort to protect his quarterback, and open holes for his running backs? And isn't he proud of the fact he gets away with much of it? What National Hockey League player hasn't clutched and grabbed with such abandon when the referee isn't looking that it appears he is mugging someone, or smeared the face of his opposite number with his glove just to make a subtle and frequently unseen—and unpenalized—point? What National Basketball Association forward hasn't bulldogged a guard or forward just to get a rebound or set a pick, even if the rules say he cannot? That sort of approach, quite frankly, is a huge part of all those sports.

But it is not part of golf. The rules there are expected to be followed closely, whether they are during a Saturday morning match among friends or the final round of the Masters. There is no room for fudging, and to turn your nose up at the rules of golf is to turn your nose up at the game itself. And there is no glory for the one who cheats. Rather, he faces only ridicule and humiliation if his transgressions are found out—and lots of sleepless nights, unless, of course, he has no conscience at all.

To appreciate that difference between golf and other sports, think about this friend who took up golf as a young boy and went on to become one of the better amateur players in the New York Metropolitan area. He was a terrific athlete who excelled in football and baseball, and part way through his teens, he got interested in golf. He took a few lessons and picked up the sport so quickly that he soon joined his high school team. On the 1st hole of his first match in his first-ever competition, he sliced a ball into the woods and went in there with his partner to find it. The boy quickly located the ball and thought nothing of picking it up from the ground, wiping it off with a towel and then sticking it on a tee he has placed in the ground. And not surprisingly, his partner was horrified.

"What in the world are you doing?" he asked, amazed that someone could break so many rules in such a short time. And the young man was not the least bit taken aback. "No one is watching," he replied. "What does it matter?" His friend shook his head. "It matters a lot," he said. "This is golf. You can't cheat in this sport the way you might in baseball or football."

Another thing that sets golf apart from other sports, and makes it such a special game in my view, is an extension of that ethic and the fact it is about the only one played without umpires of referees. Sure, officials are available at all professional tournaments and major amateur competitions to help interpret the rules. But they are not there necessarily to ensure that the golfers don't cheat. That's up to the players themselves, who are expected to call their own penalties, no matter the consequences.

They do not call it the royal and honorable game for nothing.

Not too long ago, a friend forwarded me one of those e-mails we all get so often, with a series of statements meant to put golf in perspective relative to other sports. I do not know the original author of those writings, so I cannot credit him or her. But I was intrigued with the points raised, most of which dealt with golf as a spectator sport, and I thought by reprinting some of them in this chapter, I could give further credence to the thought that golf is a very unique game.

For the most part, professional golfers get paid in direct proportion to how well they play. They are entrepreneurs to the core, and old-fashioned capitalists who rarely demand to renegotiate contracts, usually arrange and pay for their own transportation between events, and don't insist that taxpayers fork out money to build the courses on which they play.

As a rule, pro golfers are not behaviorally challenged. You do not read stories about them ending up in jail each week as you do with so many other sports. They do not kick dirt at other people or jump into the galleries and start pounding on spectators who give them a bit of grief. The occasional John Daly marital flare-up notwithstanding, you do not get a lot of police blotter copy from the golf world. And about the worst thing you ever hear a golfer do during an event is swear after a bad shot or slam his club head into the ground.

You can hear birds chirping on a golf course during a tournament. Go to a football or baseball game, and you'll find you need earplugs with all the rock music played between breaks in the action. Plus, golf tournaments do not need scantily clad cheerleaders and furry mascots to keep fans interested and entertained.

In their prime, Arnold Palmer, Jack Nicklaus, and other golf stars shook your hand and said they were glad to meet you. In his prime, Jose Canesco wore T-shirts that read "Leave Me Alone."

From a recreational standpoint, golf is in a class by itself. For example, what other sport allows you to spend four hours in a beautifully bucolic setting with friends, enjoying all the while an intensely satisfying camaraderie? What game affords you the opportunity to bond with fellow players in such an efficient and pleasurable way? Where else can complete strangers from all walks of life come together, and even in the absence of a common language become friends after a mere 18 holes? You can further business relationships on the golf course with relative ease and build friendships. You can relate to business moguls who dine with kings and prime ministers when they are not trying to learn the vagaries of this wonderful game, and you can get up close and personal with the guy who repairs your car or mows your lawn when he isn't out on the links. I have teed it up with folks in Morocco where our only common tongue was Arabic (and my vocabulary in that one is almost as limited as my short game skills) and struck up connections in the process that continue to this day. I have learned how to say, "It's good," in French, German, and Italian. I have walked on courses halfway around the world and felt totally comfortable with the other members in my foursome after only a couple of holes. Our only common bond was golf, but it was a strong one, and it sustained us through our rounds, and our time in the 19th hole afterward.

What other sports allow for that? Tennis? I don't think so. Ultimate Frisbee? Not a chance. Bicycling? It's hard to take anyone wearing one of those advertising-emblazoned Lycra jerseys seriously, let alone talk to him.

I recently returned from a fabulous golf trip with three friends, and we wondered one night at dinner: where else in our lives do we have the occasion to laugh as much as we do over the period of a four-hour round? And we could not come up with an answer. We also marveled at the fact that the four of us, ranging in years from 36 to 71 and in handicaps from 3 to 14, could have such competitive matches over the long weekend we spent together, even as we mixed up the teams each day.

And speaking of that jaunt, is there any other sport so conducive to going on the road? No one I know takes basketball trips together, traveling to various playground courts around the country so they can get in some games at different locales. But golf does that to those who like to tee it up. In fact, some of the best times you can have on a course, and in a bar afterward, come with those sorts of treks, with clubs and friends in tow.

Golf is also very good at bringing the generations together, and I know I am not alone when I say that my father and I were probably most at ease on a golf course together than anywhere else. And it was where he and I were able to finally get close before he sadly passed away roughly two decades ago. I often see as many as three generations of the same family playing in foursomes together, and my roster of regular golfing partners runs the gamut from my 16-year-old godson Owen to friends of my parents now in their 80s.

How else would we all spend time like that together if not for golf?

The game gives you such variety on the courses we are able to play, and they are not only naturally beautiful, and in many cases architecturally brilliant, but can speak to the history of the game, whether in the form of holes modeled after the great ones in Great Britain or in the history that was made there by professionals and amateurs who had played those layouts before. I mean, there is nothing like teeing it up at a place like Chicago Golf Club or the National Golf Links and seeing and feeling the superlative design work of Charles Blair Macdonald and Seth Raynor? And who hasn't gotten shivers when they walked down the fairways of a Winged Foot or Augusta National or Bethpage Black and thought of what Arnold or Jack or Tiger did in a particular situation on those very places?

Golf gives you the opportunity to play with caddies, another anomaly in sports, and whether they are grizzled veterans trying to make a living or young kids hoping to save a few bucks for college, it is always fun interacting with someone who is part psychologist, coach, partner, and humorist. And some even become your friends.

My good friend and frequent golfing partner John Akers often talks about the robustness of golf for all the things it brings those who play it, and he says it is a game of many layers and intricacies, characteristics that set it head and shoulders above any other recreation. I have no doubt he is right, and it is those aspects of the sport I try to focus on whenever I get a little irked at one of those knucklehead members who provide so much fodder for the pieces I write about club life. They may not see the game as clearly as I feel I do or appreciate its finer qualities and nuances. But I am heartened to know that as difficult and seemingly overbearing as they and their actions sometime seem, they are very much in the minority. Most people I know truly get what it is all about, and they are the ones that sustain golf—and help to make it so great.

ABOUT THE AUTHOR

JOHN STEINBREDER is an award-winning journalist with more than twenty years' experience and the author of six books, including *Golf Courses of the U.S. Open* and *Golf Rules and Etiquette for Dummies*. In addition to being a senior writer for *Golfweek*, he contributes to a number of other magazines, including *Met Golfer*; *Sky*, the Delta Air Lines publication; and *Departures*, the American Express Platinum card periodical. He is former reporter for *Fortune* magazine, a former writer/reporter for *Sports Illustrated*, and has written for a number of publications over the years, including the *New York Times Magazine*, *Forbes FYI*, *Time*, the *Wall Street Journal*. He is a longtime golfer who carries a USGA handicap index of 3 and has played at clubs and resorts throughout the United States as well as in Scotland, Ireland, England, Spain, Morocco, Switzerland and Australia. He lives in Easton, Connecticut, with his daughter Exa.